pre**conceived**

All rights reserved. © 2022

First printing: 2022

ISBN-13: 9798846978294

Each individual author is the sole copyright owner of their Work and retains all rights to their Work except for those expressly granted to Zale Mednick in this Agreement.

To the extent a separate copyright attaches to the Anthology as a collective work, Zale Mednick is the copyright owner of any such copyright on the Anthology as a collective work.

The views expressed in the articles reflect the author(s) opinions and do not necessarily reflect the views of the publisher and editor. The published material is published in good faith. The editor and publisher cannot guarantee and accept no liability for any loss or damage of any kind caused by the content of this book.

No part of this document may be reproduced, sold, stored in or introduced into a retrieval system, or transmitted, in any form or by any means (electronic, mechanical, photocopying, recording or otherwise), without the prior permission of the copyright owner.

Also available for Kindle.

preconceived

challenging the preconceptions
in our lives

edited by zale mednick

Contents

Introduction 9

Perception

There's No Such Thing As 'Normal' Skin 15
Strippers 17
The Surprising Effects of Men's and Women's Beauty 20
Ageism: Is Happy Birthday an Oxymoron? 22
Gender Diversity 25
Embrace Failure 27
Fighting the Fear of Public Speaking Failure 31

In The Beginning

Circumcision 39
Keeping Children Safe Means Letting Them Take Risks 43
Birth Order 46
A Classical Education 49
Home School 52

Worldly Truths

Philosophy 59
(Don't) Trust in Science 61
On Historical Accuracy 64
The Middle Ages 68

Sex, Love and Relationships

The Sexless Relationship 73
Polyamory is Not for Everyone, and Neither is Monogamy 77
Polyamory: Not Just One Thing 80
Selling Sex 82
Sexual Violence and Prevention 86

Social Systems

United States Military Service 93
Politics of Food Imagery: A Food Photographer's Dilemma 97
The New Corporation 100
What You Don't Know About Gun Policy 104
Zap the Generational Gap 108
Immigration 113

Animals

The Pet Paradox 119
Primate Art 122
Dinosaurs 125
Veganism 128

Parenthood

Infertility 133
The Baby Decision 136
Regretting Motherhood 139

Historical Figures

A Jewish Jesus 145
Napoleon 149

Karl Marx..153

Crime

On Death Row..159
In Prison for Murder 164
Indigenous Injustice..169

Mind and Body

Yoga: Not Just Exercise...175
Hypnosis 178
The Boxer..181
Japanese Culture: The Space Between the Stems...................185

Unwell

Depression 191
My OCD 196
The Opioid Crisis 201
Dopamine Nation 205
HIV: My Fabulous Disease 209
COVID Rehab 212

In The End

Psychiatric Illness and Medical Assistance in Dying 219
Life Extension 222
Grief...226
Six Feet Under..228

Conclusion..231

Donations 232
Acknowledgements 233

Introduction

Zale Mednick

In many ways, each of our lives is a blank canvas, an empty template that we get to decide how to fill. If afforded the liberties of living in a democratic country, we have the freedom to choose our own path in this world. We get to decide how we want to experience life and how we navigate the sometimes overwhelming plethora of choice in our modern age.

But despite this apparent freedom to choose our own path, do you ever feel like you are simply going through the motions? I know I do. For all the self-empowering talk of charting our own courses in life and forming our own unique opinions, I've often wondered if that is how I truly live.

There are so many embedded societal expectations that most of us tend to follow, perhaps without even realizing it. Think of the general path in life to which many of us subscribe: a typical classroom education in our younger years, a subsequent college or work experience, a string of monogamous relationships until we find 'the one' and get married, a stable career often entailing nine-to-five work hours, becoming a parent and raising our kids, and eventually retiring in our older years and spending time with our grandkids.

While there is nothing wrong with such a path, perhaps the critical point is that each of these steps should be a conscious choice, not a foregone conclusion. Are you having kids because you truly want to become a parent, or have you simply reached the age when having kids is the natural next step? Are you in a monogamous relationship because it reflects your authentic views on love and romance, or have you just never considered the alternatives? Have you stayed in the same career for the past fifteen years because it still fits with your true goals and desires, or is the notion of a complete pivot this far into your life too far from the norm of a typical life trajectory?

Beyond the aforementioned paradigm that dictates *how* we should live our lives, we are often indoctrinated to certain viewpoints that shape the way we view the world. From a young age, we are exposed both to practices we take for granted as normal, and social and political opinions that become so ingrained in us that they are tough to ever shake. It can feel almost impossible to form pure and uninfluenced opinions later in life, when certain perspectives and belief systems have so strongly taken hold of our psyches for so long. Is being a sex worker actually immoral, or have we just grown up being told that anything sex-related is taboo? Is circumcision just an innocent cultural ritual, or is it a potentially harmful form of genital mutilation? Is veganism really so extreme, or is it the routine practice of processing and eating animals that is actually the extreme?

In 2019, I started the podcast *Preconceived* while at a juncture in life. I was finishing my training as an ophthalmologist, a career I enjoy and continue to practice full-time today. But as I entered practice and embarked on this next stage of my life, I couldn't help but wonder, "Am I living the life that is authentic to me, or am I following the preordained path that society has encouraged me to follow?" Now that my schooling was officially coming to an end and I experienced a new sense of freedom, it was one of the first times I actively wondered whether I'd been filling the canvas of my life with the colours, patterns and designs I truly wanted.

What followed, and continues to this day, is one of the most fulfilling journeys of my life. Over the past three years, I have interviewed over 150 people who have had the bravery to share their own unfiltered truths on the podcast. The goal of *Preconceived* is to challenge the preconceptions that shape how we view the world and the paradigms by which we live our lives. Each episode of the podcast explores a different topic about which people tend to have preconceptions. Episodes have covered themes related to relationships, politics, medicine, philosophy, history and many other aspects of society and culture. The podcast has been recognized by the Quill Podcast Awards as Best Society and Culture Podcast of 2021 and The Most Innovative Podcast of 2022.

What follows here is a collection of stories, thoughts and beliefs of over fifty of the guests who have joined me on the podcast. Each author was asked the following question: "In regard to your own area of expertise, what is the greatest preconception people tend to have?" We make presumptions and form opinions on pretty much everything we encounter, and, like the podcast, the following vignettes seek to open our eyes both to new viewpoints on topics we may already have strong opinions on, and those we've barely considered at all.

The goal of this book is not to convince you of anything; in fact, the opinions expressed in this book are oftentimes at odds with each other, reflecting the authors' varying perspectives. The intention of this collection is simply to open your eyes and challenge your own beliefs about the world and the life you are living.

If there is one thing I have learned over the past few years, it is that changing the ways we think can be easier said than done. An idea might resonate with me, or a conversation might change my opinion, but because certain views and stories are so entrenched, it is often tough to truly internalize those new outlooks and make any active changes in my life. But I've also come to realize that that *too* is okay! Perhaps the mere act of exploring and acknowledging our preconceptions is the first step to becoming better, more open and adaptable versions of ourselves.

Perception

There's No Such Thing as 'Normal' Skin
Strippers
The Surprising Effects of Men's and Women's Beauty
Ageism: Is Happy Birthday an Oxymoron?
Gender Diversity
Embrace Failure
Fighting the Fear of Public Speaking Failure

There's No Such Thing As 'Normal' Skin

Jessica DeFino

Jessica DeFino is a freelance beauty reporter whose work has appeared in the New York Times, Vogue, Allure, *and more. She writes the beauty-critical newsletter* The Unpublishable.

No matter what your skin looks like right now, it is normal. No matter what. Acne? Normal. Wrinkles? Normal. Oily, dry, flaky, dull? All exceedingly normal.

Skin is *supposed* to react to the world around it. That's kind of its whole thing. The skin is a go-between for your internal and external environments; it's your body's built-in communication center. After all, what better way to get your attention?

Sometimes these attention-grabs are life-saving: breaking out in hives lets you know you're having an allergic reaction. And sometimes the skin's attention-grabs are more low-stakes: dark circles could be a sign that you need more sleep. In any case, normal skin—healthy skin, skin that does its job—is *reactive* skin. (Of course, genetics plays a big part in how or even *if* you as an individual will be affected by a particular trigger.)

So, if all skin reactions are normal and healthy, why do we avoid going out with friends, taking pictures of ourselves, or even just participating in life during a flare-up? Because beauty culture systematically breaks down self-esteem and installs shame, so that it then can *sell* us 'confidence' in the form of products and procedures.

For instance, the concept of skin types? It was made up by a beauty brand founder in the early 1900s. Helena Rubenstein first classified skin as 'normal', 'dry' or 'oily' as a marketing campaign to sell face cream. *That's* when people started to see totally normal features of the skin—oil, dead skin cells, blemishes and lines—as somehow *ab*normal. This misinformation spread and shaped the entire beauty industry, including the field of dermatology.

Or, in 1938, the founder of L'Oréal bragged that his product marketing approach was to "tell people they're disgusting, they don't smell good, and they're not attractive." Why yes, that *is* psychological manipulation. And yes, it's the foundation modern beauty marketing is built on. The idea that skincare products and procedures will 'fix' your 'flaws' and make you feel beautiful, happy, whole and worthy is everywhere.

Because we have collectively internalized this messaging, sometimes these things *do* deliver a confidence boost—but it's important to realize that beauty products can only replace the confidence that beauty standards stole.

The next time you feel like you're having 'a bad skin day', try to remind yourself that this feeling isn't yours. It's been strategically solicited by an outside force as a sales tactic, and you don't have to buy in.

Strippers

Paige Cole

Paige Cole is the founder of the Rainmaker Institute of Coaching & Healing, the creator of the RICH Method Coaching Certification, an OG million-dollar stripper, trainer of NLP and hypnosis, podcast host, author, and speaker. Paige believes that, with a little guidance, ambition, and a solid game plan, you can tailor your situation and vision to manifest the vibrant and energized life you've been craving! She lives, leads, and coaches through the principles of unwavering self-belief and confidence.

"She must have daddy issues."

"What a whore!"

"Does she have any self-respect?"

"She is taking the 'easy' way out."

"She must be a single mother or have drug problems…"

"She must not have a brain."

When you think of strippers, what stigmas, stereotypes or judgements come to mind? These are only a few of the judgements I have experienced over my thirteen-year career as a stripper.

To me, it's literally wild to see how harsh, negative and degrading people's opinions can be regarding someone who chooses a legal profession (yes, legal—we have to have a professional license to be an adult entertainer).

To be honest, for YEARS I was terrified of telling people I was a stripper for fear that they would look at me differently, treat me unfairly and not respect me.

I am an online coach and was positioning myself as a mindset and manifestation coach. I never spoke a word about stripping. The thing is, though, my business wasn't making any money at that time. In 2019, I decided to say, "FUCK THAT!" and I did what I call 'coming out of the stripper closet'. That's when everything shifted for me. My business took off and I stepped into my role (at that time) as a stripper business coach, coaching strippers on how to run their dancing business like a six-figure company, manifest more money honey, and build businesses outside the club!

I decided to embrace who I am and what I do. I decided to look at all the benefits stripping has provided me with, the lessons I learned and the entrepreneurial skills it gave me. Coming out of the stripper closet was the best thing that ever happened to me.

I'll leave you with this.

A love letter to all my strippers, hustlers and money makers:

I hope you remember to never be humiliated by your vastness or ashamed of your self-expression.

Do not be afraid of other people's opinions of what you do with your life.

Do not be concerned if someone doesn't agree with the fact that you dance.

You will keep shining...

…and you will not apologize for your light.

You can be a stripper and still be spiritual AF.

You can dance naked on stage for tips and still be a respected businesswoman.

You can give lap dances and still have an insane amount of self-love.

You can sell nude photos and videos and still have more self-worth than someone with a 'normal job'.

You can be celibate and still be a sex goddess.

You can have multiple partners and still be wholesome.

You can be sexual / sensual / erotic and still be one of the most brilliant women in the room.

If I can leave one thing in your heart today, it is to be kind to yourself.

To love yourself in entirety.

I love you, I see you.

The Surprising Effects of Men's and Women's Beauty

Daniel S Hamermesh

Daniel S Hamermesh is Distinguished Scholar in economics at Barnard College, professor emeritus at the University of Texas at Austin and Royal Holloway, University of London, and Research Fellow, Institute for the Study of Labor and the National Bureau of Economic Research.

In modern society, both men and women seem to be much more obsessed with women's looks than they are with men's looks. While people do care about men's appearance, the concern seems much less central in our thinking. Based on this obsession with women's looks, one would assume that there would be a stronger correlation between a woman's looks and her success compared to the role that beauty plays in a man's success.

In reality, though, looks don't have a bigger effect among women, at least not in all the areas we think of as indicating success. In studies that now cover a number of wealthy countries and one middle-income country (China), differences in looks among men cause bigger percentage differences in their earnings than do differences among women. Taking all this research together, women whose looks are judged by onlookers as being in the bottom seventh earn about 12% less than women whose age, education, race, location, and many other characteristics are the same but who are good-looking enough to be viewed as among the prettiest third. By contrast, when comparing the same groups among men, the good-looking guys earn about 16% more each year than men who are among the worst-looking. Thus, beauty has bigger effects on men's pay than on women's pay.

There's another area where differences in women's looks do matter a lot more than men's—dating and marriage. A woman in the top third of looks marries a man who has one more year of education than the husband of the average woman in the bottom seventh of looks. In the United States, an extra year of school leads to about 10% more earnings per year. To the extent that the good-looking wife shares in her more educated husband's extra earnings, she is better off. Guys' looks have no relation to the earnings ability of the women they marry (although better-looking men are slightly more likely to be married than bad-looking men).

With these different effects, why do we think that looks—and differences in beauty—are predominantly a women's issue? Why do we have this apparently mistaken preconception about gender differences in the role of beauty? The reason is that women care more about their looks *per se* than do men. A study of beauty and happiness in four countries showed that, among equally well-paid women, differences in looks produced larger increases in good-looking women's satisfaction with their lives—in their happiness—than do differences in men's looks.

Even though looks matter more on jobs for men than for women, in most societies it is women's looks that people focus on. That being the case, it is not surprising that good looks make women feel much better about themselves than they do among men—and that bad-looking women may feel cursed by their looks.

Ageism: Is Happy Birthday an Oxymoron?

Rachael Stone, PhD

Rachael Stone is an academic ageing enthusiast residing in Toronto, Ontario, Canada. She has dedicated her career to optimizing medical education for students and healthcare professionals in the domains of gerontology and preventive health behaviours.

Another year older, another year wiser. That's what 'they' say, right? There is no doubt that gaining wisdom is a positive stereotype of aging, but these tenuous wisdom pearls are often tied together by a ubiquitous string of negative age-stereotypes. Negative age-stereotypes and ageist practices are dominantly asserted within Western culture and, ultimately, we embody these both consciously and subconsciously.

You may believe you are impervious to such negative stereotypes, but robust research theories (see Rebecca Levy's seminal 2009 work, wherein Stereotype Embodiment Theory came to life) and decades of empirical evidence within social and behavioural psychology realms would prove otherwise. Bottom-line, negative age-stereotypes are bad for our health on every level—socially, physically, physiologically, psychologically—and we become hyper-aware of these implications in very specific instances (i.e., Happy birthday! ... ?). Age stereotype embodiment is a slow burn, much like life itself, with origins at a very young age. (Think back to your favourite movies as a child—what characteristics did the villains have versus the heroes? See my personal favourite, *The Little Mermaid*, wherein protagonists Ariel and Eric, portrayed as youthful royalty, are being tortured by the antagonist, Ursula, who is portrayed as a vile older sea creature. Perhaps more recently, see *Moana*, wherein the hero is a spirited younger adult and her grandmother is portrayed as 'the village kook' with suggestions of senility. These are just a few of many, many examples within animated and non-animated media that dichotomize attributes based on perceived age, and I implore you to view these depictions with a more critical lens). Age stereotypes and ageism place unfair limitations, not only on older adults in our society, but on every person's ability to live to their fullest potential, and devalue us as individuals.

Ageism as a recognized form of systematic discrimination was coined in 1969 (shout out to psychiatrist Robert Butler). In the 50-plus years since the inception of this notion, combatting ageism has progressed minimally compared to other forms of discrimination that continue to weave the fabric of present day 'wokeness'. In fact, many remain unaware that ageism is even a 'real' form of discrimination and, despite ageism being embedded into current judicial precedents, it remains a rather casual social practice.

The last few years have presented a unique time in human history, accompanied by an intense and expanding spotlight on unjust inequities, more than ever before. We have generally claimed to be the most self-reflective and realized version of society that has ever existed; progressive beyond bounds that previously felt immutable. And yet, ageism remains underacknowledged and often dismissed in the pursuit of an acceptable form of unjust social power. For example, let's briefly explore a recent episode of the reality television show, *The Bachelor* (season 26). This episode featured contestants engaging in a comedy roast of one another in the hope of gaining the attention and affections of an eligible suitor. As part of this activity, two contestants teased each other based on their relative older and younger ages, insinuating these chronological differences would make them both unbefitting of finding 'love' on this television show. This example highlights elements of both ageism and reverse-ageism (unjustly infantilizing/dismissing those we perceive as younger, which in turn often fosters further opposition and ageist practices towards those perceived as older). Oh, and in case you were wondering, the 'older' and 'younger' contestants were, respectively and chronologically, 31 and 23 years of age. While this 'age issue' became a prominent highlight of the comedy roast, no other socio-demographic features from any contestants were used as the foundation for comedic material. From the aforementioned example, in addition to a bevy of previous and recent portrayals within wildly popular media formats, it is clear that publicly highlighting an individual's socio-demographic features in any way has become definitively unacceptable—unless the focus is on one's chronological age.

We ask someone their age because our brains desperately crave information to determine the most successful social practice for interactions. So, what can we truly derive from learning one's chronological age? Simply put, it allows us to posit a false sense of shared experience based on time, and subsequently acts as a generational *divide* in guiding where those shared experiences begin and end.

But let's take a step back. Maybe it's worth deconstructing the abstract foundation wherein ageism and related stereotypes are rooted—ageism is essentially discrimination against time. Blink twice if you are aging right now. Chronological aging is one of the only features every single person in existence shares. When we say, laugh, or hear age-stereotypes without opposition, we are doing so at our own expense. Until ageism catches up to other civil rights movement paradigms, I say good luck to us all.

Gender Diversity

Jeremy L Wallace, MDiv

Jeremy L Wallace is a professional speaker, consultant, and author of Taking the Scenic Route to Manhood. *Jeremy speaks to students, non-profits, and groups of many sizes, encouraging each to lean into their authenticity, embrace personal growth, and work towards becoming an advocate and ally to the LGBTQ+ community.*

As an author and professional speaker, I have had the privilege of sharing my lived experience as a transgender person with many different individuals, groups and organizations. Some are beginning their journey of inclusivity and understanding, others are fine-tuning their open and affirming practices and culture, and many are somewhere in between. Yet a common preconception runs through them all—that the measure of a 'successful' transition is to 'pass'. This suggests that a person like me, who transitioned from female to male, should now look, act, and be accepted as a male, without any remnants of a feminine identity. Or the opposite for those who transition from male to female. But that can't be farther from the truth. Because the accurate measure of transition is when the individual, however they identify or present, is happy in their own skin, regardless of what others may think or see.

For me, being transgender means that I do not identify as the gender I was assigned at birth—that's it; nothing more and nothing less. The fact that I chose to pursue gender-affirming treatments or procedures does not elevate my transition above anyone else who is trans or non-binary. It was a personal decision I made, regardless of any outside factors, and was/is not necessary to identify as trans. What it comes down to is this: we are all on our own journey of becoming our true selves, no matter how we present, act, or identify. Everyone wants to live authentically without having to justify or explain our identities. So, the most important thing to remember is that *we* get to define who we are and how we live our lives; that is the true measure of success.

Embrace Failure

Dr Michael Nightingale

Dr Michael Nightingale owns and operates a dental practice in Toronto, Canada. However, during the COVID-19 pandemic he had to temporarily close his doors, which, surprisingly, gave him the opportunity to explore some of his other passions.

Growing up, I was a kid who was paralyzed by a fear of failure. For a long time, I avoided certain activities in my life even though they intrigued me, because I didn't think I'd be any good at them. Despite loving photography, it was years before I bought myself a camera; it took another few years before I actually took that camera on a trip, out of fear that the photos I took wouldn't be any good, or a waste of time. Despite an interest in skiing, I stuck to snowboarding for twenty years because that's what I was comfortable with. I guess you could say that for a long time I found a way to 'stay in my lane' to avoid any potential situations that might set me up for failure.

However, as I matured into my late twenties and early thirties, I came to a realization about my fear of failure when trying something new. My realization was very simple: "You *will* fail." Of course you will fail. Why would you be good at something the first time you try it? Nobody is! Instead of worrying about the failure, I began to embrace it as the inevitable first step of trying something new. Try something, fail (obviously), learn what you did wrong, and try it again.

When the pandemic struck, I was forced to temporarily close shop at my dental office. Like so many other professionals, my day-to-day life changed drastically as I was forced into quarantine. While this wasn't ideal, I also viewed it as an opportunity to really immerse myself in some of my hobbies. Over the past decade I have considered myself something of a 'hobby enthusiast', enjoying a fairly random array of interests. Having said that, I'd never really been afforded the kind of time that presented itself in the pandemic, where I could really focus on something other than my job.

When the pandemic started, I had a few hobbies in mind that I'd always considered immersing myself in if I had an unlimited amount of time. I contemplated teaching myself the piano, learning Mandarin, or further honing my skills to train bonsai trees. Ultimately, I decided to go all in with a hobby I'd casually picked up since before the pandemic: pasta-making.

I had been making pasta from scratch at home over the last couple of years, just as something fun to do on the occasional weekend. Initially, I'd been tentative to even dabble in the hobby, as it felt a bit overwhelming: all the equipment, ingredients, variety of recipes, etc. But, one step at a time, I gradually developed some pasta-making skills. Within a few months, I'd become reasonably skilled at making a few different types of pasta. When the pandemic hit and I suddenly had all this free time, I decided, against my traditionally hesitant nature, to go all in and see if I could really take my pasta game to the next level.

Pasta-making entails making your own dough with some combination of flour, eggs and water, letting it rest and sit, and then shaping the pieces individually by hand, one noodle at a time. With all this time on my hands, I was able to study YouTube videos, read cookbooks and test out new techniques and, ultimately, I taught myself over fifty shapes of pasta. For fun, I chronicled my progress on Instagram (@nonna_nightys). Gradually, a few friends and family members started asking if they could try some pasta. My first thought was no—

because I don't know anything about packaging and transporting food products—but then my wife and I started to look into it. Eventually, word started to spread, and people were offering to pay me to make pasta! This was by no means something I had anticipated, but I was really enjoying it and had no other pressing plans. One thing led to another, and we unintentionally found ourselves in the midst of an entrepreneurial experience. After batches of trial and error, I was able to learn the best way to take orders, make pasta, dry it properly and package it appropriately, and I arranged a curbside pick-up schedule (remember, it was deep in COVID). I was making pasta for about eight hours a day, seven days a week.

The doorway into 'trying something new' was wide open. Every move we made was uncharted territory for us and the fear of failure evaporated. The question wasn't should we or shouldn't we make a website, it was "OK, it's time for a website." We built our website, created a customer service department (my wife), and our tiny little pasta-making operation kind of exploded.

After about 3-4 months, when I was finally given the okay to return to work, it was bittersweet because I was currently in the process of purchasing the equipment to sterilize and can my own tomato sauce to sell with the pasta. It got to the point where I knew my first batch of tomato sauce was going to be a failure, but I had zero doubt I would be able to learn from my mistakes and make it work.

The truth is—it was an absolute blast. I've always loved cooking, but I never anticipated I'd be working as a full-time pasta maker, living some remote out-there dream. Even though I was cooking out of my home in Toronto, I felt like I was as authentic as a true Italian chef working in a pasta shop in Italy. Sure—there were tons of unknowns. I'd never run a business before, never had to source ingredients, design branding, shop for packaging solutions, coordinate orders and payments, or manage a website and social media account. Sure, I'd made pasta in the past, but never on a scale close to this, where I had to worry about filling tens of orders a day for months on end, let alone the most important concern of whether the product was even any good! I mean, *I* liked what I made, but it's a different story when people are actually paying for it. But that was part of the fun—the 'jump in' mentality that I had from the start, despite not knowing where any of this was going or how it would turn out.

I think the 'cure' for my fear of failure was the simple idea of starting small. Aim low. Very low. Learning something new takes one step at a time. Don't set out by learning Beethoven, becoming fluent in Japanese or making Uova da Raviolo (egg yolk stuffed inside a ravioli—which, of course, I learned how to make).

Aim low because you ***will*** fail. But anticipate the failure, and then there is nothing left to fear.

Master that step and then prepare to fail at the next one.

Fighting the Fear of Public Speaking Failure

Eli Gladstone and Eric Silverberg

Eli Gladstone and Eric Silverberg are the co-founders of Speaker Labs, a public speaking training company based in Toronto, Canada. Eli and Eric started their careers as business professors at the Ivey Business School (Canada's premiere business program) and spent a number of years working in Toronto's thriving tech sector. Today, these best friends and co-founders train some of the world's top companies including Shopify, Google, RBC and Entrepreneurs' Organization.

Failure sucks. There's no sugar-coating it. The problem is failure is inevitable. That's life. And while failure stings, the real danger is letting the fear of failure suffocate your pursuits.

Failure exists in all aspects of life, and public speaking is no exception. That said, there is one quality that makes public speaking failures feel notably crushing. A public speaking failure isn't just a screw-up... it's a screw-up *at scale*.

Public speaking is one of the most valuable skills in life but communicating in front of a crowd with the ever-present threat of public humiliation can feel as daunting as climbing Everest.

So, how can you learn to fight the fear of public speaking failure so you can crush your next high-stakes presentation?

The answer stems from a common mistake many of us are prone to making—the mistake of confusing continuums for binaries.

People often view things as black and white—binary. Zero or one. Right or wrong. But reality is almost never that basic. Instead, reality often exists on a continuum. Black and white on the extremes with countless shades of grey along the middle.

When it comes to public speaking, it's easy to get tricked into viewing success and failure as binary. Either you succeed at public speaking or you fail. However, dig a little deeper and it's obvious that success and failure in public speaking are not binary metrics—both occur along more nuanced continuums. There are *degrees* of success and *degrees* of failure.

The continuum of public speaking failure is huge. It spans from flubs as trivial as mispronouncing a word to errors as egregious as shouting racist slurs at your audience (think Michael Richards, aka Kramer from *Seinfeld*, in his regrettable 2006 stand-up show).

At Speaker Labs, we like to place public speaking failures into three different categories. We call them ***The Three Ms of Failure***:

Moment Failures

Message Failures

Major Failures

By becoming more conscious of these distinct types of screw-up, your relationship with public speaking fear will change.

Moment Failures

Some failures are so brief they barely last a moment. These are tiny screw-ups like fumbling a word, mispronunciations, briefly blanking on a thought, using improper grammar, amongst others. Often, these failures are so miniscule they go unnoticed by your audience. They are fleeting and easily forgotten.

Moment failures are nothing to be wary of, but because people feel a need to be 'perfect' when under the spotlight, these flubs can feel harmful. It's easy (and common) for people to misconstrue them as something disastrous that their audience will hold against them forever.

The reality is that not only are moment failures nothing to be afraid of, they actually present fantastic opportunities to endear yourself to your audience. When you flub something small and own it, it allows people to see your humanity. It simultaneously shows vulnerability and confidence. It's a magical combination.

Message Failures

Unlike *moment* failures, which have paradoxically positive results, *message* failures can have actual consequences. Sometimes people don't just screw up a word here or there, but rather screw up the whole message of a presentation. Perhaps the presentation is too confusing for people to make sense of, the idea misses the mark with the audience, or the audience is bored and stops listening. Regardless of the reason, the end result is failure and the objective of the presentation is missed.

Message failures actually have negative consequences because they lead to missing the intended result. Much like moment failures though, message failures don't warrant such extreme aversion. They're not the ideal outcome, but they're not as bad as we allow ourselves to believe. There are two main reasons.

First, the negative consequences are short-lived. Sure, screwing up the message hurts, but the damage is always short term. The black-and-white view is that if you screw up the message of a presentation, the audience will hate you forever and shun you from society. Of course, screwing up the message of a presentation doesn't culminate in such a devastating eventuality.

Second, message failures are great learning experiences. They can help you grow, as long as you're willing to reflect on what didn't work. Often, we find that when people experience a message failure, they become even better public speakers. They've experienced the very thing they're terrified of and, with enough accurate reflection, they can see that it's nothing to be that concerned about. Message failures are worse than moment failures—there's no doubt about it—but while they sting at first, they are wonderful teachers if you allow them to be.

Major Failures

The most severe type of failure is what we call *major* failures. While rare, it is possible to pass the threshold of *moment* and *message* failures and enter the domain of truly harmful outcomes. Major failures occur when your public speaking goes so wrong that it has the power to derail your life.

These failures are far more than passing bloopers, bombed presentations, or presentations that didn't result in a desired outcome. In the most extreme major failure cases, people lose their jobs, get blacklisted from their companies, industries and communities, and have permanent stains on their reputations.

Major failures are dangerous, but they're also unlikely. They almost never happen!

When someone experiences a legitimate major failure—where their public speaking is so atrocious that it results in disgrace—there is often more than poor public speaking at play.

A good example is Bill Clinton. On January 26 1998, Bill went on live TV as the acting President of the United States and publicly lied to the people of America about having had an affair with Monica Lewinsky. Months later, he admitted to the affair and was eventually impeached—the largest failure a POTUS can experience. Bill Clinton did a lot of amazing things during and after his presidency, but he will always be remembered in part for lying on a global stage, for breaching his marital vows, and for being impeached.

That said, there is something essential to note about him lying to all of America. If you watch the video, you'll quickly notice that Bill's public speaking was actually phenomenal. It was powerful, engaging and clear; yet it was disastrous in its eventual result. It had nothing to do with the quality of his public speaking or even the idea he was trying to communicate. It had everything to do with the fact that he was deliberately lying while acting as the world's most prominent leader. His was more a failure of moral gumption than a failure of public speaking.

Major public speaking failures are almost never a result of poor public speaking. They're usually the result of poor decision-making in front of enormous audiences by someone who possesses significant authority and influence.

Here's another important note. Despite the tumultuous nature of major failures, they are not fatal. They often humble you and help you recalibrate what matters in life. Even Bill Clinton has moved on from his global blunder. He's had a wonderful life, career, and relationship with Hillary since his turbulent misadventure of the late 1990s.

Major failures are dangerous, no doubt, and it's worth trying to avoid them, but even they can be overcome. On top of that, they are beyond rare. They have real consequences, sometimes rather harsh ones, but they are so improbable that for most people, they're not worth considering.

Does your average presentation in business and life really present the possibility for a true major failure? Probably not.

So, ultimately, how can you overcome the fear of public speaking failure?

It's simple.

Stop measuring failure as a binary, and start seeing the continuum with more nuance.

Failure isn't fun, but failure isn't fatal.

Moment failures humanize you.

Message failures teach you.

Major failures humble you.

See the gradient. Confidence awaits.

In The Beginning

Circumcision
Keeping Children Safe Means Letting Them Take Risks
Birth Order
A Classical Education
Home School

Circumcision

Brian D Earp, PhD

Brian D Earp is a Senior Research Fellow in the Uehiro Centre for Practical Ethics at the University of Oxford, Associate Director of the Yale-Hastings Program in Ethics and Health Policy at Yale University and The Hastings Center, and Associate Editor of the Journal of Medical Ethics. *Brian's work is cross-disciplinary, following training in philosophy, cognitive science, psychology, history and sociology of science and medicine, and ethics.*

Growing up in Seattle, in the Pacific Northwest of the United States, circumcision wasn't something I thought much about. I did, at some point, come to understand that penises came in two main varieties, so to speak—circumcised (foreskin removed) and not circumcised (foreskin intact). Among my male friends, some were circumcised, and some were not. If I had a preconception, it would have been that circumcision was a common practice that probably didn't make much of a difference one way or another to a person's life.

I have since learned that the 'commonness' of circumcision depends on where you live. Even in the United States, where it remains a majority birth custom, rates differ from region to region. The Midwest has pretty high rates, around 80-90% in some states; the West Coast has lower rates, down around 20 or 30%. But all these percentages are much higher than in the countries of Europe, say, where circumcision is mostly confined to religious minorities—Muslims and Jews, primarily—and isn't otherwise a common cultural practice.

The fact that circumcision might be controversial, then, really only hit home for me when I moved to England for a master's degree around 2010 and then started working at Oxford. Most British people, like other Europeans, find it hard to believe that circumcision is routinely practiced in the United States—that is, even outside of religious communities. They simply don't understand why anyone would cut a healthy baby's genitals if they didn't believe that God explicitly commanded it. Up to that point, I hadn't fully understood just how much of an outlier the United States is when it comes to circumcision. It is, in fact, the *only* so-called 'Western' country that circumcises a majority of infant boys for non-religious reasons.

This peculiar cultural distinction ends up being reflected in opposing opinions between American and European doctors—even, as it turns out, with respect to seemingly straightforward matters of medical and scientific fact. In 2012, the American Academy of Pediatrics (AAP) came out with a policy saying that the health benefits of circumcision outweigh the known surgical risks. But soon after, a response was published by heads and representatives of European medical societies saying that the AAP analysis was flawed, possibly due to cultural bias, and that its headline conclusion was false. If anything, they suggested, the risks of the procedure outweigh the benefits, especially if you consider non-surgical options for promoting health and hygiene.

This perplexed me; both groups of doctors were looking at the same scientific literature but were coming up with opposite conclusions. Clearly there was more going on here than just a dispassionate evaluation of empirical data. Instead, circumcision is a complex issue that touches on competing cultural values, conceptions of medicine and ethics, and debates surrounding gender and sexuality. How we interpret empirical data and assign significance to it depends on all those factors and more.

Much of the debate surrounding circumcision centres on what

constitutes harm. For its part, the AAP didn't seem to consider that the foreskin itself—the part of the penis removed by circumcision—might have any value in its own right. Basically, they assigned it a value of zero. Then they asked themselves, what kinds of benefits might follow from removing this part of the penis, assuming there are no surgical complications? Europeans, by contrast, take a different approach. They understand that the penile foreskin is very similar to the female labia and clitoral hood, in being made up of sensitive erogenous tissue that protects other parts of the genitalia. They therefore see it as having an intrinsic worth. To justify excising such valuable tissue, then—especially without the consent of the affected person—would require a major health benefit that was necessary for that person's well-being before they became capable of consenting, and which also couldn't be achieved in any less invasive way than by a surgical operation on their sexual organ.

The main benefit of circumcision in childhood that the AAP came up with was a reduced risk of getting a urinary tract infection (UTI). The data that support this claimed benefit are contested, because they don't come from randomized control trials, but rather, relatively messy correlational studies with a number of potential confounds. But suppose the claim is true. You can't just look at the relative risk of getting a UTI if you're circumcised or not; you have to look at the absolute risk as well. And here the claim starts to unravel. UTIs are not very common in boys, whether circumcised or not, so you would have to do about 100 circumcisions to prevent a single case. And yet, that same case could be treated non-surgically, with antibiotics, which is how it's done in girls (who get UTIs much more frequently). Given that there are effective, non-surgical alternatives, both for preventing and treating UTIs, how much weight should be assigned to this claimed benefit? One plausible answer is "very little".

In contrast, the risks of performing a circumcision can be significant. Not only are these risks the person wouldn't otherwise be exposed to, they are tightly concentrated on a part of the body that most people go out of their way to *shield* from risk throughout their lives. Circumcision involves bringing a sharp object into contact with the genitals. One hopes that the surgeon cuts off exactly the right amount of intended tissue and that there is no mistake. But mistakes do happen. Importantly, the magnitude or importance of a risk is not just how likely it is to happen in absolute terms, but how bad it would be for the person if it happened. While serious complications—such as removing too much penile skin, causing painful erections later in life; or accidentally cutting off part of the head of the penis—are assumed to be statistically rare in the hands of a skilled practitioner, they nevertheless happen from time to time. And when they do, they can be devastating for the affected person, hounding them for the rest of their lives.

When surgery is medically necessary, and so can't be avoided or delayed without putting the person's life in danger, a certain amount of surgical risk has to be tolerated. Alternatively, if someone *consents* to surgery—as in the case of certain 'cosmetic' procedures, like labiaplasty—the risk is something they take on for themselves. In the case of routine or religious penile circumcision, however, there is no medical emergency, and when done to babies, there is no consent. Exposing a child to surgical risk under these conditions is therefore hard to justify.

Keeping Children Safe Means Letting Them Take Risks

Dr Mariana Brussoni

Dr Mariana Brussoni is a developmental psychologist, director of the Human Early Learning Partnership, faculty member in the Faculty of Medicine at the University of British Columbia, and investigator with the British Columbia Children's Hospital Research Institute. Her research investigates child injury prevention and children's risky play: https://brussonilab.ca.

"Be careful!"

"Not so high!"

"Stop that!"

Those of us who have spent time with children at play have heard these exclamations from well-meaning adults and may even have spoken them ourselves. We can be overwhelmed with worry that our children will get hurt or that others will think we're a bad parent for letting our child take risks. Childhood wasn't always like this. Many of us have fond memories of childhoods spent outside, hanging out with friends in our neighbourhoods, parks and wild places, making up the rules as we went along, with minimal (if any) adult supervision.

We need only reflect on our own play memories to realize how valuable these experiences can be and how they can shape our lifelong health and development. Playing outside is not the same as playing inside. When children are allowed to play outside the way they want to play, risk taking becomes a natural part of play—climbing, running, play fighting, building structures. They move more, sit less and play longer. They make their own goals and figure out the steps to attain those goals, helping them build executive function skills. They learn about the world and themselves, build resilience and develop their social skills. They also learn how to manage risks and keep themselves safe.

My decades as an injury prevention researcher have left me well aware of things that can go wrong and how to prevent them from happening. But as a developmental psychologist, I have also seen the effects of keeping our children too safe. Preventing our children from exploring risk and uncertainty means they don't have the opportunity to experience how to manage the strong emotions that come with these experiences—fear, exhilaration, joy, failure, defeat. They don't figure out what they are comfortable with doing, what their limits are, how capable they are of managing challenges and the consequences of those experiences, both positive and negative. They learn to rely on adults to make decisions for them and flounder when there aren't adults to tell them what to do. They become afraid of risks and avoid them; they find it hard to manage the anxious feelings that come with life, and their self-confidence suffers.

These days, we approach parenting in a bid to make childhood as risk-free as possible, thinking we are keeping our children safe and setting them up for success. Nothing could be further from the truth. We are preventing children from developing the basic tools they need to thrive, and we are also stripping them of opportunities to learn how to manage these risks when they become more serious and consequential.

Injuries are the leading cause of death for children in Canada. This fact can be scary to hear and helps us justify our restrictive approach. But we need only dig a bit deeper into these statistics to realize our fears are not justified. The leading killers are motor vehicle crashes and suicides. We don't let our children walk to school because we're afraid they'll be hit by cars or kidnapped. Yet being a passenger in a car is the most dangerous thing a child can do. And being kidnapped is so rare that you're more likely to win the lottery. We've seen a massive increase in mental health concerns and suicides. Yet we rob children of the opportunities to build their self-confidence, independence and resilience to be able to manage the basic challenges of life. In short, keeping children safe means letting them take risks.

The biggest favour we can do for our children is to let them play. There are three key ingredients necessary: Making sure children have lots of **time** every day to play outside. Ensuring they have access to fun outdoor play **spaces**. This can be as simple as making sure there are lots of loose parts (e.g. sticks, stones, water, cardboard boxes) they can use and letting their imagination shape the play. And giving them the **freedom** to play how they choose. Our job is to manage the really serious hazards that can cause severe injury, but then we need to get out of the way and let children play.

For parents struggling with letting go, my lab has developed the OutsidePlay.ca online tool to help parents manage their fears and develop a plan for change so their children can have more opportunities for play. Change can be as simple as counting to 17 before stepping in. Parents are often amazed by how capable their children are when given the opportunity to manage things on their own.

Birth Order

Catherine Salmon, PhD

Catherine Salmon is a professor of psychology and director of the Human Animal Studies program at the University of Redlands. Her research and teaching interests include birth order and family relationships, male and female sexual strategies, and the use of popular culture as artifacts in the study of human nature.

The Preconception: When researchers say birth order effects exist, it means that birth order is the *only* factor that matters to the behavior or trait in question.

The Bigger Picture: The reality is that no one factor is typically the *only* one influencing complex psychological traits such as personality and intelligence or behavioral outcomes with regard to relationships either within or outside the family. Is birth order related to personality? There are lots of studies that suggest it is and that traits such as conscientiousness are stronger in achievement-oriented firstborns while openness to experience may be greater in laterborns. However, those personality traits are also influenced by genes (as seen in twin studies) and perhaps other aspects of the environment, both within the family, such as number of other siblings, and outside the family, such as peers. It's not just how parents invest in their children and have expectations for them that influences their development, but also parental genes that are passed on that influence a wide variety of traits, including intelligence and personality. Sibling dynamics and how a child is parented contribute to the family environment in ways that cannot be underestimated. We are all intimately and inextricably tied to our parents and siblings, and these ties influence our past and impact our future.

Your DNA determines how tall you'll be (in combination with environmental factors like nutrition), or whether you'll have curly or straight hair. But, if your older brother is a basketball player and your younger one is a soccer star, there's a greater likelihood of you turning to tennis or rowing, even if you're 6ft 2in tall or love dribbling. And if you do choose the same sport, you're likely to approach it with a different strategy. For example, Sulloway and Zweigenhaft examined risk-taking and participation in different sports as well as the performance of brothers who were both in the major leagues. Their results indicated that, while in general lastborns are more likely to participate in high risk sports, when brothers participate in the same sport the younger brother is more risk-taking in their strategies, such as base stealing in baseball. Why? Family dynamics.

Why is it that two siblings can be as different from one another as are pairs of children selected randomly from the population? One behavioral genetics review concluded that environmental influences are the key—in particular, environmental differences between children in the same family, such as birth order. When researchers talk about the roles of genes and environment in development, environment gets broken into shared and non-shared environments. Part of the point we are making is that, despite the shared family environment of socioeconomic status and culture within a family, there is a significant non-shared aspect to family life as experienced by siblings. They receive different amounts of attention and investment from parents (even when the parents are trying to be equitable it doesn't always turn out that way) and they experience the competition from their siblings very differently. In addition, they often interact with different peers outside the family.

Early in life, we adapt our behavior in an effort to compete for our parents' time, affection and resources. Openness to innovation and to being different (typically laterborns) and strong identification with existing power and authority (typically firstborns) are behaviors learned during our early years as part of this sibling competition for parental attention and investment. If big sister Ashley gets all the kudos for her figure skating, and little brother Tom's every babble is considered delightful, middle child Tricia will—perhaps unconsciously—be busy finding a way to draw some attention to herself by being different from her siblings. In this way, siblings and parents shape the niches children occupy. Specific niches and traits may thus be characteristic of specific birth orders but again, they are also influenced by the sex of each child, number of siblings, and sibling traits, as well as parental expectations for specific children.

There are lots of factors (biological/genetic as well as environmental—some shared, some not shared; both within the family and outside the family) that interact and combine in different ways to influence who individuals become, their occupational choices, and relationship styles. Birth order is one of those factors; and although birth order often yields patterns when examining many different traits/behaviors, it is also important to acknowledge the wide range of variation in those traits among individuals of the same birth order. This is why some middleborns, such as Bob Hope and Johnny Carson, can appear very similar in many ways, while others, like Donald Trump and Desmond Tutu, can appear to be very different.

A Classical Education

Susan Wise Bauer

Susan Wise Bauer is a historian, educator, and farmer. She is the author of the History of the World *series,* The Well-Educated Mind, *The Well-Trained Mind, and* The Story of Western Science.

For the classical philosophers, education came down to what it meant to be human. The purpose of education was not to figure out how to do stuff or to figure out what we need to know. The purpose was, "Who are we supposed to be?"

We have largely gotten away from this mission, with the primary goal now being to collect as much knowledge as possible. It's been really fascinating for me to watch education expand over the past thirty years. When my mom was homeschooling us in the 1970s, she didn't have many choices of curricula since there wasn't that much out there. Since then, the whole field has boomed, and there are so many things you can study. There are so many subjects, there are so many approaches, which has resulted from the general explosion of human knowledge since The Enlightenment. In the 17th century, you could be a well-educated person by learning most of what was in print in English because it was such a smaller field of study. You could know a lot about science and history, and you could have a sense that you had mastered the available field of knowledge. That's where we get this now impossible idea of being a Renaissance Man. We use that term to describe someone who has mastered all the basic knowledge, but with the abundance of knowledge that now exists, it is simply impossible to meet the impossible threshold of a Renaissance Man. The idea has emerged that in order to be educated, there is a core set of things that everyone has to know and agree are important to know. This is completely antithetical to the idea of a classical education.

When you look back at the philosophers of The Classical Age, the foundation of education was, "What is a whole man?" and "What is a fully human man?" In both Plato and Aristotle, we see this expression of the idea that an educated man, a developed and whole man, is one who can accumulate information, look around the world, and gather what he needs to know. He can evaluate it for himself, think for himself critically about whether to accept it and how to prioritize it, and then make up his mind about it, have an opinion about it, and express that opinion with grace, fluency and persuasiveness. That's a really fascinating concept of what it means to be human. What is really central to this classical education is the idea that you're not fully human until you can articulate what you think. It's all about how we interact with the world around us, how we take it into ourselves, and how we express it back out again.

In *The Well-Trained Mind*, we teach those three steps. First, how do you gather and find information? Second, we focus in on the whole critical thinking and logic part of the equation. It's not just important to gather information, but to look at where it came from. How do you know that it's true? What are the biases behind the people who are presenting it to you? Who are you getting your information from? And, in the third and final phase, we really start to home in on what is called 'rhetoric', which is persuasive self-expression. Only once you have gathered information and evaluated it can you have an opinion about it.

One of the hallmarks of this process is that each of these three stages is age appropriate. Elementary students don't have a lot of critical ability. They'll shout at you, tell you they don't want to go to bed, but they don't have the mental maturity to be persuasive. They can try to exercise blunt force, which is why they have tantrums instead of explaining themselves. As they move into the middle grades, the logical and critical thinking parts of their brains really start to develop, which is why middle schoolers can be so incredibly annoying. They're not going to just take your word for it anymore. They need explanation. As students move into high school and college and really begin to develop a strong sense of who they are as people, it becomes incredibly important for them to be able to articulate what they believe, what they think, and give their opinions.

As we walk students through these three stages of becoming an educated person, we're basing it on age-appropriate maturity. One of the hallmarks of a classical education is that we don't ask kids to do something before they are ready. We don't ask third-graders to write persuasive essays, for example, which, unfortunately, was part of the common core writing standards, which was completely age inappropriate. Alternatively, we *do* ask high school students to have opinions, not just to regurgitate facts that they learned from a textbook, which, unfortunately, also happens in a lot of school systems.

We have seen over the past few years, especially more recently in discussions over the vaccine, that people don't know how to perform these three steps of collecting information, analyzing it, and forming an opinion. People just go straight to opinion. They don't know where the trustworthy sources for information are. People too often skip the two steps that should happen before you have an opinion. That is not an educated response.

Home School

Josh Steimle

Josh Steimle is an entrepreneur, speaker, and Wall Street Journal *and* USA Today *bestselling author. He lives in Arizona with his wife and three children.*

Like most kids in the United States, I attended a public school from the time I was five years old until I graduated from high school at the age of eighteen. In addition to those thirteen years of firsthand experience as a student within the government-run education system, both my mother and father began their professional careers as public-school teachers. My father taught for two years, decided it wasn't the right fit for him, and became an optical engineer, working for NASA on projects like the Hubble Space Telescope.

My mother taught for a few years until she had children. I was the last of the four she had, and when I was in sixth grade, she began to take on substitute teaching jobs, then became a full-time teacher again, and went to graduate school part-time to earn a master's degree in education. She taught full-time for around fifteen years until she retired.

When my mother began to teach again, I became her *de facto* teacher's aide. I assisted her in grading papers, cleaning up the classroom, and dozens of other miscellaneous tasks. I saw how much extra time she worked (she was always the last teacher to leave the school each day) and how much of her own money she spent on school supplies (I went on many trips to school supply stores with her, and she told me how the school didn't give her enough money to do what she wanted).

It wasn't until I was sixteen years old that it occurred to me to question what I knew about education. That's when I met a girl who had skipped two years of high school.

"Wait, how did you do that?" I asked her.

"I got ahead and tested out," she replied.

I didn't know such a thing was possible. And yet, even with her example, it still didn't occur to me that I could do the same thing. I was too steeped in the system as I knew it to think about changing my course.

After high school, I attended a year of college. College was different from high school. While some classes were required, I had a lot more space to choose what I wanted to study, and many options to fill that space.

After my first year of college, I served two years as a missionary in Brazil for The Church of Jesus Christ of Latter-day Saints. This was a life-changing experience in many ways, not least that it led me, upon my return to college, to change my major from art to business. There was just one problem—I had failed virtually all my math classes since the 7th grade. Now, for the first time, math couldn't be ignored. I couldn't do what I wanted to do without it.

I chose to retake my math classes—all of them, starting with pre-algebra, the 7th-grade math class that began my string of math class failures.

Since these were remedial math classes, which most students didn't need, they were offered in a math lab in which there was no teacher, only a tutor who could help me as I worked through coursework on my own. As soon as I finished my coursework, I could take tests, and as soon as I passed the tests, I could finish the class. In other words, I could move at my own pace rather than needing to wait for anyone else.

As I dug into the coursework, I made a startling discovery—algebra was much easier than I remembered it. I breezed through an entire nine months of 7th-grade math in two weeks and got an A. I still had plenty of time left in the semester, so I started the next class. Two weeks later, I finished that one, also with an A. I started the next class, finished it, and the next, and so on. In that first semester, I took a total of 25 college credits (12-15 credits is a normal load) and got all As (except for one A-). In just a few months, I completed five years of math classes. It was easy, and I enjoyed it.

What changed between my public-school years and college? The difference between my two experiences with math was so stark that I seriously wondered if my brain had physically changed in a way that made math easier. Ultimately, I settled on a primary reason math became easier, which was that I saw a purpose for it. When I thought I would be an artist, math seemed like a waste of time. When I changed my major to business, it became necessary.

However, I can't discount the different educational formats. In my junior high and high school classes, I had to learn with everyone else and go at the speed prescribed by the teacher. In college, while catching up, I could move at my own pace. That, in and of itself, made learning math more interesting to me.

This experience prompted me to question the standard K-12 system in the United States. Was it really best to have a class of thirty or so students with a teacher at the front of the room instructing them? Why weren't students encouraged and enabled to progress at their own pace? Why was the system set up the way it was?

A few years later, I took the GMAT test to get into a graduate business program. The test is divided into two parts, quantitative (math) and verbal (reading and writing). The test is adaptive, meaning the more questions you get right, the harder the subsequent questions provided by the computer program that administers the test.

Although I had caught up on math, I didn't become a wizard at it, by any stretch. My quantitative score was good enough, and no more. However, on the verbal part of the exam I missed just one question. Just one question kept me from getting a perfect score on the reading and writing portion.

You might think I got perfect scores in K-12 English classes, but I did almost as poorly in those classes as I did in my math classes. Perhaps I studied verbal more while preparing for the GMAT? Actually, I barely studied for either quantitative or verbal.

The skills I used to do well on the verbal portion of the GMAT were almost entirely self-taught. My mother had taught me to love reading from a young age, and I grew up voraciously reading everything I could get my hands on. While in college, I read well beyond what was assigned to students, soaking up magazines, business books, and anything else available. When I took the GMAT, the answers on the verbal portion were intuitive.

Again, my experience caused me to question the predominant forms of education. I had outscored the vast majority of those who take the GMAT, largely through self-directed learning that had no structure and followed no formula. Could it be that this natural form of learning, where someone studies whatever they feel inclined to, was superior to all the complex learning systems smart people had developed?

More years passed, and my wife and I had children. As those children approached the age of five, we considered our options. By this time, I had read John Taylor Gatto's book *Weapons of Mass Instruction* and had soured on traditional educational environments. I felt the public school system was broken beyond repair, but I didn't feel all that much more favorable towards private K-12 schools or the higher education system.

When our oldest child turned five, we enrolled her in a public school, mostly because we had just moved to Hong Kong and wanted her to learn Chinese, something we definitely couldn't do at home since neither of us knew the first thing about it. However, we withdrew her before the year was over. The negatives outweighed the positives and we felt she was better off at home, with us.

After that, we decided to homeschool our two children for the next several years. I became a strong advocate for homeschooling, and we continued to homeschool 100% of the time until we adopted a third child, who was older than our other two. Our third child was fourteen years old and raised in China. The last three years before we adopted her, she was in a boarding school. Homeschooling was as foreign to her as speaking English and eating breakfast cereal. After she had been in our family for a few months, she begged to go to school, and we relented and allowed her to. She has thrived there. More recently, another of our children asked to go to school, and she now goes half-time, while homeschooling half-time. She's also thriving in the traditional school environment. Our third child continues to homeschool, and I can't imagine him thriving in a traditional school.

I used to think the traditional K-12 model of childhood education was the only option. Then I believed homeschooling was the superior method. Now, I'm not so sure. The only thing I can say with much certainty is that every child is different, and what works for one child may not work for another.

Maybe your child will do best in a traditional school environment. Maybe they'll do better homeschooling. Maybe they'd do even better in a self-directed learning environment like a Sudbury school or an Acton Academy. If there's any preconception I'd ask you to reconsider, it's the one that says education has to look a certain way.

Worldly Truths

Philosophy
(Don't) Trust in Science
On Historical Accuracy
The Middle Ages

Philosophy

Eric Weiner

Eric Weiner is author of the New York Times *bestsellers* The Geography of Bliss *and* The Geography of Genius, *as well as the critically acclaimed* Man Seeks God *and his latest book,* The Socrates Express: In Search of Life Lessons from Dead Philosophers. *His books have been translated into more than 20 languages.*

When I told people I was working on a book about philosophy, they would get this pained look on their faces. It was as if I'd just asked them a difficult calculus question, or they were having some flashback to their undergraduate days and the intro to philosophy course they'd been forced to take. The truth is, philosophy often gets a bum rap.

At its core, philosophy is about wisdom. I would say that in some ways everyone is a philosopher, though perhaps an *accidental* philosopher. There are many moments in our lives, especially over the last couple of years, when we pause and ask ourselves, "What is the purpose of this world?" or "How can I find meaning in my life?" Those are philosophical impulses. The only difference between being a true philosopher and having those impulses is the intentionality involved in those thought processes. A true philosopher actively seeks out wisdom, rather than relying on chance that the important lessons will simply come to us as we stumble through life.

Most of us believe that we might accidentally get a tidbit of wisdom here and there, but wisdom itself is seldom taught in schools. Knowledge is taught in schools, but wisdom isn't, really. One might derive wisdom through their family or friends, but it's often happenstance or accidental. That seems wrong to me.

One qualm that people have with philosophy is this notion that it is all about asking questions. There is a view that philosophers only care about posing questions, but don't actually care about the answers. I think that is a misconception; I think philosophers *do* care about answers. They probably care more about the questions, though, because the questions we ask reflect the way we frame a problem, and *that* is what determines the answers we come up with.

Philosophy is practical. I realize that might sound shocking and absurd to a lot of people, but it was initially conceived as the most practical thing one could do in Ancient Greece. The Stoics, for example, really wanted to be involved in politics, so their philosophy was correspondingly designed to make the world a better place. The philosophical schools of ancient times were competing against each other. But they were not judged by the long treatises they wrote. Rather, they were judged by the practical results that their philosophies achieved. Contrary to popular thought, philosophy is not just about *examining* your life. Philosophy is about accumulating wisdom so you can better *live* your life.

So why did I write a book about philosophy? I did it to help recapture and recover philosophy back to its original intent, the love of wisdom.

(Don't) Trust in Science

John Asher Johnson

John Asher Johnson is a professor of astronomy at the Harvard-Smithsonian Center for Astrophysics at Harvard University. His primary area of study is the detection and characterization of planets orbiting other stars.

During and since the pandemic, there's been a notion floating around American society, and quite possibly the world, that it's really important to just 'trust in science'. This notion of 'trust in science' started showing up on bumper stickers during the Trump administration. I'm absolutely no fan of Trump, but I was also no fan of 'trust in science' as some oppositional stance to take. As a scientist myself, I think this idea that one should just trust science is akin to someone who is buying a house saying, 'trust in hammer', or 'trust in screwdriver'.

Science is a tool that human beings have at their disposal for trying to understand the way the world works. And to say that you *just* trust this tool is, at best, grossly missing the point and, at worst, a societal meme that is positioning people to blindly trust authority.

For me, this all prompts the question 'What is science?' What exactly is it about science that people trust? Is it trust in the scientific process? Or is it that people trust scientists themselves? From talking with people both in and out of the scientific community, my impression is that what people actually trust is the consensus view amongst scientists that is purported to be based upon scientific results.

Trust in the scientific consensus, however, presupposes that science actually *advances* through the beliefs of the majority. There is this distorted view that has taken shape that what matters is a consensus view, as if the truth of the universe is arrived at by the majority of scientists all agreeing on what that truth is. In reality, though, science stagnates on consensus. The only way that science has ever truly advanced is when a minority of the scientific community puts forth a hypothesis that challenges the mainstream majority, a paradigm that challenges the status quo, one that the majority is often reluctant to entertain.

The dominant view of science not only espouses something to be true but, unfortunately, often sets the confines of the questions that can be asked. There is only a certain subset of questions that is considered relevant by the scientific community at large: questions that fit within the parameters of established scientific thought. Sure, less established scientists can feel free to ask whatever questions they'd like to, but if the questions too boldly challenge the dominant thinking, they often run into a structure that is set up to push back.

Take, for example, the peer review process by which all scientific manuscripts are assessed prior to publication. The peer review system itself draws from respected scientists who generally conform to the dominant paradigm. Society trusts that such reviewers will be open-minded to questions that challenge the status quo. But that is putting a lot of trust in ordinary people to suspend their preconceptions of scientific truths and make room for potentially ground-breaking discoveries that shatter much of conventional scientific wisdom.

It can be easy to forget that many of the most influential scientists of the past century were essentially rogue thinkers, people on the margins of mainstream thought. Albert Einstein, Carl Sagan and Richard Feynman challenged the status quo; they were outliers on issues both inside and outside of science. They did *not* represent the majority. Yet, over the past twenty years or so, a societal view seems to prevail that scientific consensus and the views of the majority are all that matter. But if we simplify science to conforming to the majority's point of view, we risk marginalizing some of society's greatest thinkers. We risk ostracizing the next Einstein. Further, conforming to the majority fosters a scientific culture that does not truly encourage free thought, nor give credence to transformative questions that might yield groundbreaking results.

It is more important now than ever for us to acknowledge that society has become overly conformist to a science based on majority thinking. We must recognize the limitations of ceding to the popular view and simply *trusting* in science as it is currently practiced. It behooves us to consider that the scientific majority is most often influenced by pharmaceutical interests, industry funding agencies, university-driven agendas, and many other factors that are completely divorced from authentic scientific process.

As a scientist, I *do* revere science. As an astrophysicist, I respect the scientific process. But I also think that science should not be placed upon a pedestal, in some sacred shrine above questioning. The public at large needs to understand the truth behind science, including its inherent flaws, biases, and tendency to follow the path of least resistance. So, before you put that bumper sticker on your car that proudly claims, 'Trust in science', ask yourself if you really understand what science is and what that bumper sticker truly stands for.

On Historical Accuracy

Aaron Irvin

Aaron Irvin is Associate Professor of the Ancient World at Murray State University, KY, USA. His research examines human organization, government, empire, and religion in the Roman world and in the Late Bronze Age system of states.

History traces its origins as a genre back to the 5th century Greek author Herodotus. It was he who coined the term *Historia*, meaning 'inquiry' or 'research', for his work. Herodotus presented what he saw as the origins of the recent conflicts between the Greek city-states and the Persian Empire, basing his arguments around the facts, stories and anecdotes he had gathered in his travels around the eastern Mediterranean. Herodotus' work was thus grounded in research and a gathering of absolute facts, but ultimately based on his own interpretation and presentation of those facts in order to reach a conclusion.

In crafting *Historia*, Herodotus drew inspiration from several pre-existing Greek literary genres. Individual city-states and the nearby kingdom of Lydia maintained official state annals, records of yearly events and accomplishments. Yet these annals only recorded that events occurred; they provided no analysis, commentary or interpretation of those events. It was Herodotus' innovation that began to connect events together in a cause-and-effect relationship and thereby explain how a chain of events and decisions had brought about the conflicts between the Greeks and Persians. To present these events in a compelling manner, Herodotus tapped into another pre-existing Greek genre, the Epic, the most famous examples being Homer's *Iliad* and *Odyssey*. Herodotus did not simply state that events had happened; he re-created them in his narrative, transforming historical figures into mythological characters whose lives became demonstrations of social values and cultural mores. Even the Greek gods themselves had roles to play, weaving their way in and out of the affairs of men in Herodotus' historical narratives. Herodotus likewise drew from the developing dramatic genre of tragedy in the city of Athens, pulling influences from the works of Aeschylus and Sophocles in his crafting of characters, scenes and dialogues. From the outset, History found itself as a hybrid of multiple genres, seeking to explain human events and human characters while simultaneously looking to entertain and using conventions from storytelling alongside investigative research.

As a literary genre and, ultimately, as a field of academic study, History continued to evolve into the present day. What has remained consistent is the use of a narrative to connect events together, and thereby give those events meaning and significance. This also means that History is inherently interpretative, and that interpretations between different historians examining the same subject might vary wildly. Any interpretation must ultimately be based on the available facts and evidence. Thus, while History does not in fact deal with the discovery of an absolute 'way things actually were', any historical narrative presented must account for the known historical facts in its interpretation of events. History thus presents not a singular, absolute truth, but a range of potential truths, supported by recorded events but ultimately dependent on the way those events are weighted and interpreted by the historian.

There is a tremendous amount shared between the study of History and the creation of entertainment, and it comes as no surprise that History has served as a consistent source for drama and storytelling. The Historian remains bound by the available evidence, and their conclusions and narratives must account for the available facts. Those facts might be interpreted in a number of different ways, but the Historian must justify those interpretations. Thus, as a field, History continues to shift and change, with new interpretations and new evidence emerging all the time, casting new light and shaping new narratives about the significance of past events. The Dramatist, meanwhile, remains bound by their own separate set of rules as well, conforming to the necessities of genre, of tropes, of audience expectation and performative norms, and the necessities of the chosen medium.

What then is meant by the idea of 'historical accuracy' in terms of drama and entertainment? In studying ancient Rome, we have a variety of different daily artefacts, but from locations that stretch from Jerusalem to London and beyond. We have ruins and houses and different types of buildings, all of which survive in different states from different time periods for different reasons. We even have an entire city in Pompeii, a snapshot in time buried in ash and mud. We can draw generalities and a very broad image of what life was like over an extent of time and in several places, but the more specific we get, the more clouded and questionable our historical image of the Roman Empire becomes. What, for example, can the remains of Pompeii really tell us about life in other Roman cities? How applicable is the data really? What are the limitations of our evidence, especially when we fundamentally don't know what we might be missing?

When we flip over to drama though, audiences have a very clear image and expectation of what a show about ancient Rome should look like. This image has been developed over the past century in movies and television series. The image of Rome is itself grounded in evidence, in its own way, but it is a combination of material goods, clothing and hair styles, building styles, weapons and armor, names and places, selected from the range of available evidence across time and space. Is this image accurate? Well, it is based on evidence, but more importantly for the audience, this image has solidified into something identifiable and real. Deviating from that image becomes impossible because the audience becomes lost, the scene unrecognizable, and the setting of the drama loses the tropes and dramatic imperatives that make it worthwhile in the first place.

Historians and Dramatists are both storytellers, the genres inextricably linked and intertwined with each other. While they are thus connected, they necessarily have different goals. Historians analyze and process evidence, interpreting and creating connections to explain the significance and meaning of events in a variety of different ways. There's no singular vision of the past then that Dramatists must inherently adhere to, no ultimate measurement of accuracy to demand. Rather, the question is one of possibility, of the likelihood of a character or plot given the available evidence, but simultaneously communicated in such a way as to be legible to the audience.

Studying the past, especially the ancient world, is the closest any of us will likely come to walking around on an alien planet. While it is the job of the Historian to grasp and understand the otherness of that past world, the Dramatist has the tools and the ability to communicate that otherness to an audience, and to understand how that ancient world might still tell us something about our own.

The Middle Ages

Susan Wise Bauer

Susan Wise Bauer is a historian, educator, and farmer. She is the author of the History of the World *series,* The Well-Educated Mind, The Well-Trained Mind, *and* The Story of Western Science.

The Middle Ages were invented by historians in the seventeenth century. Think about the term 'The Middle Ages'. You can't have a 'middle' unless you've got point A and point C, and you need something to come between them.

In the seventeenth century, a phenomenon was recognized by historians. In the late fifteenth and early sixteenth centuries there had been a practical, politically driven rediscovery of classical books that had not previously been accessible to the West. The West is the only culture that has a middle age. When we talk about The Middle Ages, we have to recognize that it was driven by the possibility of European scholars for the first time, in the fifteenth and sixteenth centuries, traveling into areas which had been held by Muslim kingdoms. Up until then, the Muslim kingdoms had been very unfriendly towards European scholars there. There was a lot of hostility between these Arabic-speaking countries and Western countries, what we now think of as Europe.

Up until that time, the classical Greek and Roman texts had largely been in Muslim-held countries. Arabic speakers had translated them and were aware of them well before European countries were. In the fifteenth and sixteenth centuries there were political shifts that allowed for the translation of these texts into European languages for the first time. There was huge interest from the Germans, French, English, and the peoples in what we now think of as modern-day Europe. These texts could be read for the first time, since these texts were now physically accessible.

The surge of interest in these classical texts led to a *reappreciation* of the ancient cultures of Greece and Rome. Because the texts were 'new', it was thought of as a 'rebirth' of these cultures, but only in the West since these texts had been available in Arabic-speaking countries for centuries. And we're not even talking right now about further east in Asia. Asia has no classical, medieval and renaissance periods; nothing of that sort happened in China and Japan. There's a whole different set of progressions that happened there in the 17th century.

In the 17th century, historians started to examine this rebirth of interest in classical texts. Jacob Burckhardt was probably the first Western historian to really put a name to it and call it a 'Renaissance', a rebirth. So, we have 'Classical Times' and now we have 'The Renaissance'. What Western historians then try to wrap their brains around is: we've got this whole chunk of time in the middle. What do we call it? We call it the middle! We call it 'The Middle Ages'! We call it the time between the two things we have decided are important, which is the classical world and the *rediscovery* of the classical world.

This is why the classical age became cast by Western historians as a 'golden age'. It's a historical invention. Part of really understanding what we call The Middle Ages is to try and ditch this idea that it was a big dark spot between two bright spots and look at what was actually happening!

Sex, Love and Relationships

The Sexless Relationship
Polyamory is Not for Everyone, and Neither is Monogamy
Polyamory: Not Just One Thing
Selling Sex
Sexual Violence and Prevention

The Sexless Relationship

Dr Jane Greer

Dr Jane Greer is an internationally-known marriage and family therapist, psychotherapist, sex expert, author, and host of the Doctor on Call *radio hour at* HealthyLife.net, *which features* Shrink Wrap on Call, Pop Psych, *and* Let's Talk Sex. *She is the creator of the relationship commentary* SHRINK WRAP *on what we can learn from the trials and triumphs of celebrity relationships, which appears in print, online, and on TV.*

As a marriage and family therapist, I work with many couples who co-exist within what has become known as 'the sexless relationship'. A sexless relationship is one in which there is no sexual intimacy taking place with any kind of regularity for an extended period of time, and which causes at least one of the partners, if not both, to be disappointed, unhappy or upset.

When people think of a sexless relationship, they probably imagine older couples, or couples who have been together for a very long time and now have a more 'boring' sex life. That, however, is not the case at all. Many of my patients are younger people who are just starting out in their relationships—people in their early twenties who are confused and surprised by the lack of sexual intimacy they share with their partners. I see both men and women who are not initiating sex, not looking for sexual continuity, and lack any consistent sexual connection in their relationships. There is a sexual anorexia that prevails for so many, and it can be really disappointing to so many people who unexpectedly and unwittingly find themselves in a relationship with a partner they love, but with whom they're just not connecting in an intimate way.

Underpinning 'the sexless relationship', or any relationship in general, is the misconception that maintaining a vibrant sex life is easy. Rarely does sex go easily for two people. Usually, it's an experience that needs to be navigated with intention. Couples need to define and express their mutual needs. Lovers need to learn their partners' desires and what pleases them. They need to read when their partner is in the mood or not. And because there are so many points in the course of a sexual encounter that can lead to a partner becoming upset, disappointed, or turned off by what their partner has or hasn't done, there is so much potential for withdrawal and retreat.

Sexless relationships often result from conflict in sex initiation. For example, let's say Molly tries to initiate sex, but her partner Andy isn't in the mood and says no. Molly might feel a bit hurt and upset, but she is able to get over it. But then she might come back a couple of nights later, and her attempts at initiating sex are again refused. A couple of things can now start to happen. The first is that most people take it very personally when their partner says no and experience it as a personal rejection, viewing themselves as unattractive and undesirable. The second thing that happens is they might get angry with their partner, feeling that it's unfair that their partner is the one who gets to decide when they do or do not have sex. This can then lead to a standoff, where Molly, in this example, stops initiating sex, both out of fear of rejection and resentment of Andy's apparent control of the situation. This further compounds the problem.

If you have two people with different levels of desire to begin with, and the partner who is generally more interested in sex is now retreating, the situation is set up for even less sex. Andy might misinterpret Molly's decreased sexual advances to mean she is actually *okay* with having less sex. He doesn't realize that Molly is lying in bed beside him gripped with resentment and frustration, just waiting for Andy to make a move. Molly and Andy are in totally different headspaces. Molly might want to have sex two or three times a week, while Andy is okay having sex twice a month. Now that Molly is no longer initiating, Andy thinks that Molly is on the same wavelength as him. And, frustrated with Andy, Molly will initiate even less, perhaps not at all.

Relationships can also become sexless by hurtful encounters *during* intercourse. I encourage people to speak in terms of what they want more of and not in terms of what they *don't* want. There is nothing quicker to turn a partner off than saying, "I don't like it when you go so fast," or "I don't like it when you put your tongue in my mouth." I once had a patient whose husband criticized how she French kissed, and she didn't tongue him at all for the next twenty years! All you have to do is criticize your partner's moves, and they'll stop moving. And it only has to happen once. One seemingly innocuous comment interpreted as a criticism by the other partner can lead to years of withdrawal from and anxiety about sex. Contrary to what one might think, it only takes one comment, reaction or negative sexual experience to stymie all sexual activity in a relationship. It is not the case that sexless relationships only develop slowly over long periods of time.

Sex is a process that requires work. The only place sex is easy is in the movies. In the movies, you see somebody, you meet them, you want to rip their clothes off, and you do. Women are immediately excited, hot and aroused, and sex can happen on beaches, floors, decks, anywhere. But the movies aren't real life. Sex requires work. Sex is like dancing. You have to learn how not to step on your partner's toes. You have to learn how to lead and follow. You have to learn each other's rhythms. And all of this takes trust and effective communication. Ultimately, I encourage couples I work with to communicate with each other. Without communication, it is impossible to know if you and your partner are on the same page. Communicating may not sound as fun and spontaneous as the sex in the movies, but in real life, positive communication is the most important factor in maintaining a healthy sex life.

Polyamory is Not for Everyone, and Neither is Monogamy

Dr Elisabeth 'Eli' Sheff

Dr Eli Sheff is a researcher, expert witness, coach, speaker, and educational consultant. With a Ph.D. in Sociology and certification as a Sexuality Educator from AASECT, Dr Eli specializes in gender and sexual minority families, consensual non-monogamy, and kink/BDSM. She is the foremost academic expert on polyamorous families with children, and her 25+ year Polyamorous Family Study is the only longitudinal study of poly families with children to date. Dr Eli has published four books and over 25 journal articles and chapters and is currently editing a series of books on relationship and sexual diversity.

Living in a society in which monogamy predominates, most of us grow up believing monogamy is the truest or best way to experience love and romantic relationships. As with so many things in life, it can be easy to accept the status quo and never really consider love and relationships outside the confines of the norm. Society has so romanticized the idea of a monogamous everlasting love that it isn't hard to see how many of us have been indoctrinated to believe that's the *only* form love can take.

Indeed, monogamy might be the preferred way of life for many people. But, rather than simply *assuming* we are monogamous, we might find more meaningful love and relationships if we take an active look at the options that exist to find out what we truly want.

The Bonding Project is a relationship test I co-developed that people can take to assess their preferred bonding style: one-to-one, one-to-many, many-to-many, or solo. Essentially, it's designed to start conversations and offer a way to begin to explore relationship options. Over 15,000 people at different junctures in their lives have taken the original test, including younger folks who are figuring out what style of relationship might work for them, and people already in relationships who are considering expanding the parameters. Other participants might be coming out of a relationship and reassessing what they want in their future relationships based on what worked and what didn't work in their previous romance. Still others might be in a period of self-growth and wondering if the way they've been living their lives so far is still the best way to move forward.

One of the most interesting findings we have observed is that people can get different test results when repeated over months and years. Respondents' results can vary based on their mood and mindset at the time of taking the test. Just as relationships themselves are dynamic processes, our own views on love and relationships are dynamic too. People's relationships can have a wide range of expressions, and across a lifetime it is quite common for people's relationship preferences and styles to shift or change as they age.

A lot of polyamorous folks believe people can have many kinds of different relationships that can be meaningful and important, but that don't necessarily have to look a certain way. Perhaps more important than the *type* of relationships people choose is that the type of relationship people consider is a *choice* in the first place. If that choice is monogamy, great. If that choice is polyamory, that's great too. If that choice is some other form of romantic relationship or none at all, then that is great as well. And if it changes a number of times across someone's life, then perhaps it means they are truly embracing the winds of change that can take hold in anyone as they experience all this world has to offer.

Polyamory: Not Just One Thing

Alana Phelan

Alana Phelan, known online as The Polyamorous Librarian, is an author and public speaker from the Philadelphia area. When she's not co-authoring books about polyamorous superheroes, she can be found reading books, talking about books, or working on a non-fiction book about polyamory thanks to a 2020 Effing Grant.

The biggest preconception people have about polyamory is that it's any one thing. When monogamous people ask me about my life, when people who want to open their relationships come to me for advice, and even sometimes when polyamorous people are stuck in a conflict, I find that everyone has a set idea in their heads about what polyamory is and how it's practiced.

The truth about polyamory is that it's a position from which a person can ask, "Assuming I don't have to do what society expects of me when it comes to relationships, what do I want?" With that as the starting point, polyamory plays out in as many different ways as there are people who love. A closed triad; a married couple dating separately; a constellation of loosely-connected partners, metamours and comets; queerplatonic partnerships; or a single person open to the possibility of loving more than one person at a time—these are only some of the thriving types of polyamory I've seen in my twenty-five years of knowing polyamorous people.

That said, I think everyone should ask themselves the above question, and then ask it of the people in their lives. I recognize that we are not always given space to ask, and especially we are not always given space to act on the answers. But as someone who made that space for myself and the people I cared about, and then tried my best to follow through on everyone's truth, I've had a fuller, happier life as a result. I wish that space, that safety, and those fuller, happier lives for everyone.

Selling Sex

Carly Kalish, MSW, RSW

Carly Kalish is an advocate, innovator and thought leader supporting survivors of trauma. Carly is currently the Executive Director of Victim Services Toronto.

There are a million reasons someone can enter the sex trade, just like there are a million reasons someone might become a teacher, a chef or a social worker.

Can you think of another form of work where people make so many assumptions about how or why you got there?

In this chapter, I hope to challenge two preconceptions: first, that everyone working in the sex trade has been coerced into that work; and second, that despite what we see in movies and other media, most sex trafficking is not foreign, but rather domestic, and happens to young people in communities across the world.

First, some terminology. My view is that 'sex work' is a valid form of work, just like any other job, carrying with it inherent risks and benefits. 'Sex trafficking', on the other hand, is about exploitation and coercion. It is a violation of fundamental human rights, and it is not a form of work at all. These two terms are very different, and it is dangerous to conflate sex work and sex trafficking.

It may be helpful to think about the sex trade in terms of 'the 3 Cs', which are on a spectrum. The 3 Cs are choice, circumstance and coercion.

On one side of the spectrum is choice. Many sex workers are consenting adults choosing to engage in sexual acts in exchange for some form of payment. The sexual acts are consensual and the person performing them gets to choose how the money they earn is spent.

On the opposite side of the spectrum is coercion. In these situations, someone is being exploited, tricked, or forced to do sexual acts, and a person or group of people is benefiting from exploiting that person.

The final C, circumstance, which is in the middle of the spectrum, is where many people conflate sex trafficking and sex work. Circumstance is when a person's situation is inherently exploitative, but no person is directly exploiting them. Common examples of how circumstance can exploit include poverty, addiction and mental illness.

Someone performing sex work because of their social or economic circumstances is not the same as sex trafficking, and it is, in fact, dangerous to conflate the two. Many of the sex workers I have worked with over the past ten years are sick of people wrongly assuming they are being exploited and need saving. Conversely, victims of sex trafficking by coercion are not getting the support they need because the media paints a completely inaccurate picture of what sex trafficking looks like. In fact, many survivors have told me that they didn't even know they were being trafficked because they understood trafficking to be completely different than their experience.

Sex trafficking is usually a relational crime. It happens when someone builds a relationship with you for the purpose of ultimately forcing, tricking or coercing you into the sex trade. It is often a boyfriend, friend or even a parent or caregiver who builds trust and then 'grooms' you over time. The trafficker takes time to assess your vulnerabilities; they find out what needs are not being met in your life, and then offer to meet them. The trafficker starts by taking care of you and toys with your emotions until, finally, you rely on them and *only* them for support. Whatever it is that you feel is missing in your life, they position themselves as the solution to fill it.

The second preconception about sex trafficking is that it is foreign victims being brought into another country. Data from support agencies, police and government show the majority of sex trafficking that takes place in Canada and the United States, for example, is actually domestic trafficking.

This may be an unsettling thought. For every high-profile story of a young girl brought into North America for the purposes of sex trafficking, there are dozens of other stories of young girls who are being exploited locally. Perhaps they started chatting with someone online, a guy in their neighbourhood or someone with whom they had mutual connections on social media. This new acquaintance might ask them about their hopes and dreams and really take time to get to know them on an intimate level. They then meet in real life and 'fall in love'. It isn't until a few months down the road that this new acquaintance might suggest that if only the young person could help them make some money, things could be even better. "You know—all the things I have done for you, those weren't free. You owe me. If you don't say yes, I will post the nude you sent me on social media. No one will have to know. It will be our secret. We will keep the money we save for our future together so we can buy a car and rent an apartment of our own."

Unfortunately, the number of such cases in North America is rising. Sex trafficking is one of the fastest growing crimes in Canada and the United States. Our response, however, should not be to ban sex work or push it further underground, where conditions of sex work by choice become more dangerous. Rather, the antidote is addressing the root causes of inequity and focusing on education and public health. Sex trafficking is a manifestation of inequity and is a human right abuse. It thrives where there is a power imbalance. To stop human trafficking, we need to dismantle oppressive structures and understand gender-based violence. We must empower young people to make safe and healthy decisions and equip them with tools to learn about consent and healthy relationships.

By better understanding the sex trade, we can begin to accept those working in it by choice and do whatever is possible to prevent coercive situations.

Sexual Violence and Prevention

Tim Mousseau

Tim Mousseau is a survivor of sexual harassment turned speaker and researcher. Over 450 organizations, including congressional offices, professional sports teams, international franchises, and beyond, have partnered with Tim.

If I ask any of my audiences whether they consider sexual violence an issue worth preventing, the answer I will always receive is a resounding yes. No matter the audience demographics, program context, or extent of our conversation, everyone can agree that no one should experience any form of violence or harassment.

Further, if I ask any audience if they are willing to help prevent sexual violence, the answer will once again be a yes. Overwhelmingly, the support to preventing sexual violence seems unified.

If so many people are willing to help prevent sexual violence and recognize it as an issue, why does sexual violence in every form continue to exist? Why do so many individuals, an estimated 1 in 4 women and 1 in 6 men, still experience some form of rape, assault, intimate partner violence, harassment or beyond in their lifetime?

The answer I've found is that far too many people undervalue what sexual violence entails. Though so many seem unified in stopping these behaviors, far too many different definitions of sexual violence exist. And, overwhelmingly, it seems like people only perceive sexual violence to be the most egregious of behaviors: those acts involving physical violence. Direct acts of bodily harm. The willful, predatory ignoring of consent.

Yes, egregious behaviors such as rape and sexual violence must be stopped. On the same token, until we collectively broaden our understanding of what behaviors constitute sexual violence and the harm any of these behaviors can perpetrate, we will never entirely prevent these issues.

One of the best resources I ever found was labeled 'The Pyramid of Sexual Violence'. The Pyramid of Sexual Violence breaks down different types of sexual violence based on severity, from outright assault at the top to degradation in the middle and normalization near the bottom. Defined under assault are behaviors like rape, intimate partner violence, or drugging. As you move down the pyramid, the behaviors move into categories such as the stealth removal of a condom, coercion, or groping under degradation. Then, at the bottom, for normalization, are behaviors such as catcalling, rape jokes, or offensive gendered language and slurs.

The pyramid's importance lies in recognizing that violence escalates in communities and relationships. Though there are individuals who choose to willfully engage in predatory behaviors no matter the circumstances, more often than not, sexual violence builds.

The danger is that the more our society, communities and friend groups accept those normalization behaviors at the bottom, the more permissive we are of behaviors near the top. The acceptance of sexual violence occurs gradually by degrading individuals' bodily autonomy and worth. The more that groups embrace beliefs, values and systems that normalize any form of sexual violence, the more likely it is that other behaviors will follow.

Stopping sexual violence requires more than intervening when someone acts as a predator. In fact, these moments might be rare compared to the opportunities where we can call out sexist language, educate around the danger of harmful jokes and challenge harmful beliefs around 'accepted' consent violations in relationships.

The problem is that challenging the beliefs, values and systems that normalize sexual violence can be hard work.

For example, the embrace of traditional concepts of masculinity (values such as a man's worth is tied to the sex they have, men have to be the sole providers and protectors, or men must withhold emotions to be physically strong, to name a few) correlate to a greater willingness to accept or minimize incidents of sexual violence. Talking about and removing these traditional values from our cultures involves complex work. It requires a thoughtful review of our own actions. It takes a willingness to be aware of the media we consume and how it influences us. Challenging these values means we have to look at how we are raising boys and young men. And sometimes, these challenges require honest assessments of decades-old systems that no longer benefit anyone.

This work takes time, diligent effort, and difficult conversations. It is vital, though.

No matter how much I wish there was, no one clear answer to preventing sexual violence exists. Instead, it takes significant, profound actions and changing regular habits. Preventing sexual violence requires we peer into the foundations of our world and honestly evaluate the systems that are causing harm. It requires changes to laws and policies around holding perpetrators accountable. It takes the constant adoption of new education. It takes criticism of our media, entertainment, and what we permit in pop culture. And, above all, it requires that we as individuals are more willing to examine our own habits: those beliefs, behaviors and actions we take in our own relationships and communities that lead to the normalization of sexual violence.

This is significant work. And it is uncomfortable.

Do I believe my audiences when they tell me they know sexual violence is an issue and wish to help prevent it? Absolutely. Do I also need more of them, more of everyone? Yes.

Preventing sexual violence is not a one-time moment of action in a time of immediate harm. It can be, sure. Truly preventing sexual violence, though, requires a more diligent evaluation of the systems that have brought us here, the systems that are no longer working, and how we can all play a part in preventing the normalization of violence.

Social Systems

United States Military Service
Politics of Food Imagery: A Food Photographer's Dilemma
The New Corporation
What You Don't Know About Gun Policy
Zap the Generational Gap
Immigration

United States Military Service

Alan Leggitt

Alan Leggitt served in the United States Army as an infantryman from 2004 to 2009, where he deployed to Iraq in support of Operation Iraqi Freedom. He is a graduate of Airborne School, Ranger School, and the Warrior Leader Course, and his stateside duty stations include Fort Benning, Georgia; Fort Bragg, North Carolina; Fort Richardson, Alaska; and Fort Polk, Louisiana. After leaving the military, Alan joined the anti-war organization About Face (formerly Iraq Veterans Against the War). He lives in New York with his wife Amy, his dog Fry, and his cat Oswald, where he works as a data scientist in the healthcare industry.

When I share the fact that I served as an Infantryman in the United States Army from 2004 to 2009, the most common response by far is "Thank you for your service." In the 18 years since I first enlisted, I have yet to find a reply that feels genuine. "You're welcome," implies a small favor, like holding open a door, and does not capture the gravity of those five years. Embedded within the phrase "Thank you for your service" are two preconceptions that I struggle with: one, that joining the military was a selfless act, and two, that my military service was benevolent.

On September 11th, 2001, I was a 15-year-old sophomore in high school, living in the suburbs of New York City. My stepfather was a member of the National Guard and was activated to provide security to Ground Zero in the aftermath of the attacks. At a time when I might otherwise have started thinking about what college I might attend, what field I might major in, or what career I might pursue, it suddenly felt that the most important thing I could do with my life was to defend my country from further acts of terrorism. At least, that's what I told myself.

There were many subconscious factors that influenced my decision to join the army. Besides my stepfather, my biological father, my uncle and both my grandfathers were also veterans. Military service in my family was so common, in fact, that I did not have any relatives who could explain to me the basic steps required to pursue higher education. And while I did have friends at school who were college bound, it felt safer to risk my life in a warzone than to admit that I needed guidance.

At the same time, I was struggling to accept that I was sexually attracted to both men and women. Despite the growing acceptance of the LGBTQ+ community, especially near a major city like New York, I did not feel safe exploring this part of my identity. Instead, I hoped that the military would serve as a form of conversion therapy, a proving ground where I could assert my straightness and masculinity.

The 2003 invasion of Iraq did not dissuade me from joining the army. At 18 years old, I accepted the premise that multiple predominantly Muslim countries could work together to threaten the American way of life. It didn't matter to me that these countries were more than 1,000 miles apart, nor that the United States had previously supported both the Taliban and Saddam Hussein's regime in their respective wars against the Soviet Union and Iran.

My military training was not overtly Islamophobic, but anti-Muslim sentiments were embedded in the culture regardless. Our drill sergeants regularly used racial slurs to describe Afghan and Iraqi civilians and warned us that even women and children could be employed as suicide bombers. We watched videos of Western journalists being beheaded by Al-Qaeda operatives, set to the sound of Muslim prayers. During a 'cultural education training', a Christian chaplain gave us a multi-hour lecture on why Christianity was good and Islam was false, despite the fact that there were a handful of Muslim soldiers in the audience.

By the time I deployed to Iraq in 2006, the term 'quagmire' was widely used, both inside and outside of the military. Saddam Hussein's regime had fallen, and we were in the process of 'nation building' against a tide of insurgency and civil war. Some days we met with local leaders to discuss developing public infrastructure. Other days we kicked down doors and arrested suspected terrorists, even when they were unarmed. At all times we had to be vigilant of the guerilla tactics employed by the enemy: rockets, snipers and roadside bombs, just to name a few. It did not take long before I grew to question the wisdom and morality of the war in Iraq, especially as I witnessed the egregious amount of collateral damage we left in our wake. What kept me going was not my devotion to spreading democracy, but a concern for the safety of my fellow soldiers.

When I separated from the military in 2009, I found a community of like-minded veterans called About Face (previously known as Iraq Veterans Against the War). In this community, I was able to take stock of the damage US military interventions has done across the globe; to examine the racist, sexist, Islamophobic and homophobic elements of military culture; and to be critical of the tactics used to recruit socioeconomically disadvantaged youth into the military. The About Face community was especially valuable during the Trump presidency. I learned to leverage the social capital that comes with being a veteran to protest violence against marginalized communities.

I don't hold it against people when they use the phrase "Thank you for your service," nor can I propose a better alternative. During the war on terror, the experiences of combat veterans have been largely siloed from the experiences of civilians, and it's natural for us to gravitate towards well-worn cultural scripts. I do, however, feel that we in the US need to have uncomfortable conversations about whether the money and lives we spend on militarism are in fact making the world a better place.

Politics of Food Imagery: A Food Photographer's Dilemma

Kyla Zanardi

Kyla Zanardi is a Toronto-based commercial photographer and director specializing in food and lifestyle content. When she's not shooting cookbooks or an upcoming campaign, she's hanging out in the kitchen with her partner Matt and their dog Cali.

Have you ever heard the saying, "We eat with our eyes"? Well, I am in the business of getting you to eat with your eyes AKA making food look beautiful. You know those pesky five-second ads you're forced to watch on YouTube, the ones where the cereal dances across the screen, or the epic music builds as it zooms in on a burger that is so big it's seemingly impossible to eat? Well, I make those.

For the most part, I love my job. However, there is a certain paradox that I constantly face, being both a food photographer and someone who is concerned about the future of our planet and food security. On the one hand, my job is inherently to make food insatiable, irresistible and bountiful. Perfect plump tomatoes, unblemished radishes, golden hourglass pears: the list goes on. On the other hand, food insecurity is more rampant than ever, and the constant threat of climate change forces us to think more deeply about the complex ecosystem that is food production, consumption and marketing. On a global scale, it's clear we have a problem. According to the United Nation's Food and

Agriculture Organization, a 2011 study explains that "roughly one-third of the edible parts of food produced for human consumption gets lost or wasted globally, which is about 1.3 billion tons per year."

Whether I like it or not, as a food photographer I am implicated in this debate. According to a recent study from Second Harvest, in Canada alone **58% of all food produced** is lost or wasted. Food *loss* accounts for things like the discolored (yet completely edible) apples that the farmer can't sell to retailers. Food *waste* accounts for the apples that retailers are forced to discard because they don't sell prior to their 'best before' dates, or the unconsumed food in a restaurant buffet, or the food we throw out on set. These are just a handful of examples that make up food loss and food waste, but they are the ones most relevant to my work. Other examples of food loss include labour shortages that affect harvesting crops, changes in production schedules, or contracts that result in loss of crops, etc. However, the one segment of food loss that cannot be overlooked is largely aesthetic—only certain 'grades' can be sold to grocery stores, and these grades are determined by factors such as shape, color, size and firmness. In other words, certain foods that are perfectly fine to eat are rejected purely based on their appearance.

Enter the 'ugly produce' movement. You probably think I'm joking, but I'm not. The 'ugly produce' movement was born out of a response to this very problem. Companies in the 'ugly produce' movement aim to recover food that would otherwise be discarded in an attempt to normalize and reimagine what we consider edible produce, and then sell it to consumers. In this way, non-profit and for-profit businesses have capitalized on blemished, spotted, mis-shaped and misfit fruits and vegetables. Some critics argue that while it might address food loss, it doesn't account for food waste. And while the ethics and politics around this movement are important to debate, the very nature of this work raises invaluable questions about reconceptualizing what we demand of our vegetables and fruit.

As a food photographer, I know I am part of the system that has created and upheld a very specific standard for what we understand to be desirable food. But think about *this*: that standard we have created, and that consumers have bought into, doesn't even factor in the most important thing about food: taste! Food photography is completely based on the visual, yet our visual perception has falsely become synonymous with quality and taste. The food industry thrives on the preconception that only what looks good actually tastes good.

Yes, the visual aspect of food can of course be a huge part of the dining experience, one that I enjoy capturing in photos. But if the consequence of all this beautiful food imagery is that we have come to refuse perfectly fine-tasting apples simply because they possess inconsequential blemishes, then perhaps it is time to reconsider if the pendulum has swung too far. So, the next time you're in the grocery store, standing in the fruit aisle and about to grab an apple, ask yourself what you are looking for, and why.

The New Corporation

Joel Bakan

Joel Bakan is a professor of law at the University of British Columbia. He wrote the award-winning books and documentary films The Corporation *(2004) and* The New Corporation *(2020), as well as* Childhood Under Siege *and numerous scholarly works.*

In the late nineties and early two thousands, there was a lot of popular discontent about the growing power of corporations in the global economy. Protests around the world were taking aim at corporations' growing power and impunity in a globalizing economy, and at the seeming unwillingness and incapacity of governments to do anything about it. My initial book and film, *The Corporation*, chronicled this moment, put it in historical context, and called for a robust response from democratic governments worldwide.

Over the past twenty years since that book and film, corporations have actively tried to put forth a new and reformed image centred on social responsibility. It is variously described as stakeholder capitalism, ESG (environmental, social, governance), corporate social responsibility and corporate sustainability. I think most people are familiar with the way, under such monikers, corporations have been presenting themselves as sustainable, environmentally aware, and wanting to solve global problems. There's been a lot of advertising to reflect this changing sense that corporations are actually the good guys, actors that are truly on our side to help the world become a better place. One can see it in numerous instances. Corporations supporting Black Lives Matter and voter rights in Georgia. Canadian mining companies pledging to be environmentally friendly. Major oil and gas companies taking up the cause of climate change. Just go to the website of any major corporation and you'll think you've landed on the page of an activist group. It's all about the good works they are doing around the world.

The reality, however, is very different from the image that is being portrayed. The new corporation is very similar to the corporation of old. Its essential legal structure—which demands that managers and directors always prioritize the self-interest of the corporation itself—remains unchanged. No doubt there have been some positive changes in how corporations behave, but many of the changes are more for show than anything else. One could say that the greatest transformation of the new corporation is the way it *markets* itself as an agent of social change, rather than actually *being* an agent of social change.

Corporations have been able to convince governments that because they are now the good guys, they can be trusted to self-regulate, and that regulation is therefore no longer needed; that they can take over roles traditionally regarded as governmental, like managing water systems, running schools, or tackling climate change. In essence, what they are saying is that they should be involved in governing more than being governed. But can we really trust this new corporation?

I point to numerous examples in my latest book and film, *The New Corporation*, that illustrate the dangers of such self-regulation, two particularly poignant: the Deepwater horizon explosion that nearly destroyed the Gulf of Mexico, and the 2008 financial collapse. A large body of academic and even governmental reports point to deregulation as a root cause of both crises, which led to immense devastation and destruction. As I show in the book and film, the companies responsible for these crises were also at the forefront of the new corporation movement, companies that had gone to great lengths to portray themselves as good actors.

British Petroleum (BP) was the first oil and gas company to say that climate change was a problem to be addressed. Yet despite this show of environmental support, the Deepwater horizon crisis actually resulted from the company's neglect of certain environmental and safety standards. JPMorgan Chase was another company that had branded itself on the forefront of the movement for corporate change. Yet that company ultimately had to pay 13 billion dollars in a legal settlement for its maleficence which contributed to the 2008 economic collapse. In both cases, each company had lobbied extensively for deregulation and claimed they could self-regulate. Yet, as noted, it was the inadequacy of that self-regulation that helped cause the devastation that ensued from both crises.

Perhaps one of the most clever ways in which the new corporation has been able to falsely portray itself lies in the concept of 'offsets'. Take Coca-Cola, for example. When Coca-Cola says that it has become 'water neutral', the suggestion is that they give back as much water as they use. This has become a very important part of their ad campaigns, as water has become a scarcer commodity due to overpopulation and climate change. But what does it really mean for Coke to be 'water neutral'? Does it mean that they *actually* give back all the water they use? Of course not. What it means is that they buy offsets. Here is how it works.

Let's say Coca-Cola buys twenty offset credits from an intermediary company. That intermediary company will then take that money and do things with it that are theoretically helpful in the replenishment of water. The intermediary company might invest in a program that plants trees and thus helps with water retention. Coca-Cola can then claim via their economic models that the amount of liquid in each Coca-Cola bottle is adequately being replenished via this program. Not only have economists seriously called into question the accuracy of such calculations, but there's real potential for deception. For example, what Coca-Cola doesn't mention is that its model only takes into account the water in the bottles themselves, not the huge amount of water that is used to create and refine the sugar they use, which is many-fold greater than the water in the bottles.

The whole offset system is quite deceptive from the start, and Coca-Cola is by no means alone in this. There are many more examples like this, with airlines, oil companies and other corporations claiming that they are *carbon* neutral.

The Pope, among other critics, has come out swinging against offsets, arguing that we can't simply buy our way out of doing wrong, whether that's polluting or anything else. To underline His Eminence's point, it would be ridiculous to suggest you can cheat on your spouse so long as you buy an offset that's used to help some other couple stay together by, for example, paying for their couple counselling or a romantic trip.

Beyond offsets, there are many other ways the idea of the new corporation is a myth. A lot of companies have become better at *representing* themselves as forces of good without truly becoming better. So how do we move forward? My ideas about reform are pragmatic. They are not that we need to root everything out and destroy corporations and the market systems in which they operate. At least in the short term, that is not going to happen. What I do say is that we need to reject the new corporation-spun myths that corporations' goals are the same as the goals of society at large, and that, left to their own devices, they will do good rather than harm. That is a deception, and a dangerous one. Markets and for-profit corporations need to be regulated by society rather than the regulators of society. We need to get back to the idea that the public interest and democratic governance are the ultimate goals of what we should be doing when governing society.

What You Don't Know About Gun Policy

Trevor Burrus

Trevor Burrus is a research fellow in the Cato Institute's Robert A. Levy Center for Constitutional Studies, editor in chief of the Cato Supreme Court Review, *and host of the weekly podcast* Free Thoughts *from* Libertarianism.org.

Here's something you probably don't know: between 55-60 percent of gun deaths in the United States are suicides. Gun suicide rates in the United States have been stable for some time. In 2020, for example, 54 percent of total gun deaths were suicides, which is approximately half of all suicides in general. In contrast, there was a significant and disturbing spike in gun *homicides* in 2020, up about 14 percent from 2019.

These are disturbing facts, but it is important to get the numbers right if we are going to have mature and productive discussions about gun policy.

Unfortunately, many gun-control advocates talk only about total gun deaths and ignore the important differences between suicide and murder. While all deaths are tragic, the best policies for addressing a suicide or a homicide problem are drastically different.

Lumping all gun-related deaths together allows gun-control advocates to point to a strong correlation between gun deaths and the number of guns in circulation (the 'gun stock'). Look at one of the graphs often used by the *New York Times* or Vox, and the correlation will seem clear as day: the more *guns* there are in a state or a country, the more *gun deaths* there are. And this is likely true—but because of gun suicides. Look carefully at one of those graphs showing which states are hotbeds of gun deaths and you'll see that Wyoming and Alaska—hardly epicenters of interpersonal gun violence—are strangely at the top. That's because they have both a lot of guns *and* the highest suicide rates in the country.

While there is a correlation between gun stock and suicide, there is absolutely no correlation between gun murders and the gun stock. In other words, having more guns in circulation does *not* correlate with increased gun-related murders. Perhaps one reason that gun-control advocates don't want to separate suicides and murders in the numbers is because it undermines the simple case for gun control that is so often repeated: more guns equals more crime. This is simply not true.

Take states like North Dakota, Wyoming, West Virginia, and Montana, all states with about 50 percent gun ownership rates and gun-murder rates markedly below the national average. Or states like Delaware and Maryland, with ownership rates at 20 percent or below and gun-murder rates above the national average.

True, there are many important differences between these states, primarily rates of urbanization, but the simple narrative is still complicated by these numbers. It's also complicated by nationwide stats. From 1993 to 2013, the gun-homicide rate dropped 49 percent but, during that same period, America probably added 100 million guns to the gun stock.

Internationally, the same is true. Germany, Norway, Sweden, and France have a fair number of guns—at least for Europe—yet the homicide rate is higher in Portugal, Italy, Greece, and Ireland, which have markedly fewer guns. Take all the countries of the world and graph the gun stock with gun homicides and you won't find any correlation. Basically, the graph will look random.

And while there can be good-faith disputes about these numbers—just estimating the number of guns in a country is extremely difficult—at minimum we should not be conflating suicides and murders when crafting gun policies. When activists say things like "Forty-five thousand people were killed by guns last year, so we need to ban 'assault weapons'," it borders on the nonsensical. Twenty-five thousand of those deaths were self-inflicted, mostly with pistols, and no policy focusing on the functioning of guns—e.g. magazine restrictions, banning features like pistol grips and folding stocks—will do anything to affect the gun-suicide rate.

But gun-rights supporters don't spend enough time talking about suicide either. It's more likely gun-rights supporters are gun owners themselves, or at least know gun owners, so it should be a problem they care about. Having a gun in the house certainly raises the risk of gun suicide—how could it not? It's quite difficult to shoot yourself if there are no guns around.

That doesn't mean we should be taking guns away. Some people like having risky things in their houses because they enjoy using them, such as swimming pools. Those with pools, especially parents, put in safety devices and teach their children how to swim. Gun owners who feel suicidal should be encouraged to get help, to lock up their guns, and maybe even ask friends to keep them for a while. But if they're afraid their guns will be confiscated, then they are much less likely to ask for help.

Ultimately, it's sad. There are lives that can be saved, but we spend an inordinate amount of time, money, and political capital advocating for policies that will not measurably affect the number of gun deaths. Any serious discussion of gun deaths in the United States must focus on suicides of men between 25–64—which are fully 37 percent of all gun deaths—and inner-city gun violence, mostly affecting young Black men. Pistols are by far the most common guns used in both these situations, yet policy discussions can't seem to stop focusing on AR-15s.

And while horrific mass shootings are often committed with guns like AR-15s, those shooters would have used whatever gun was available to commit their crime. Furthermore, the mayhem that can be committed with a pistol is just as much—if not more—as with an 'assault weapon.' The concealability of pistols means a shooter could blend back in with the crowd and extend the carnage. This is precisely what happened in Virginia Tech. It seems that shooters choose 'assault weapons' partially because they think they look cooler, and image matters to these murderers.

As a gun-rights supporter, I don't want to take away the pistols either. But even more than being for gun rights, I'm for rational and productive discussions rooted in facts, not panicking about whatever gun happens to scare Senator Dianne Feinstein this week. On both sides, our gun-policy discourse is rooted in ignorance, fear, and posturing, and we can do better.

Zap the Generational Gap

Meagan Johnson

Meagan Johnson (meaganjohnson.com) is a professional speaker and generational enthusiast who writes and speaks about the ever-changing multiple generations and the best practices of the organizations who employ and sell to them.

Having a 'generational misunderstanding' is nothing new. Many of us have walked away from a multi-generational interaction with less than stellar results. We are left scratching our heads, thinking, "Is this a generational issue or a personality problem?" Combined with conflicting generational information, our own generational preconceptions, and blatant generational stereotypes, it can be a challenge to forge a new path with the people of different ages in our lives.

Now, following a global pandemic, it has become increasingly necessary to address our own generational preconceptions and debunk negative generational myths.

The truth is, the workforce, and possibly your household, spans five generations. Each has experienced the pandemic through a different lens. At one end of the spectrum, younger generations are beginning their careers during one of the largest global upheavals the world of work has experienced. At the other end, an entire generation, on the precipice of retirement, is learning how to conduct business in an increasingly digital environment. It can be a struggle to find the right balance between the sometimes conflicting needs of each generation.

In this vignette, we will examine some small steps you can take to demystify some of the preconceptions regarding the younger generations.

Preconception: The younger generation wants to be rewarded for 'just showing up'.

In reality, younger people want to be rewarded for their contributions. They do have a higher desire for feedback and collaboration than preceding generations.

Feedback is my favorite word

Greater than 65% of Generation Z want weekly feedback at a minimum (preferably more).[1]

74% of Millennials name collaboration as one of the top two priorities they want in a workplace.[2]

What can managers do to create the culture of feedback and collaboration Millennials and Generation Z crave?

An HR manager I recently interviewed told me he abolished the yearly review. He said, "Young people do not care about feedback that is a year old. They care about the day-to-day relationship they have with their employer."

One tool he uses to solidify the employer/employee relationship is The Stay Interview, which helps managers understand why people stay and

---

[1] Shenton Chris, Gen Z in the workplace: Culture needs to be 'frequent feedback' focused, https://www.weekly10.com/gen-z-and-workplace-feedback/, 5/15/20

[2] 4 Workplace Elements Sure To Engage The Millennial Worker, https://www.hrcloud.com/, 4/28/15

why they leave. Additionally, it is an effective tool that allows people to feel heard and know that their opinion has value.

Some sample Stay Interview Questions:[3]

What do you like most about working here?

What kind of feedback would you like about your performance that you are not currently receiving?

What have you felt good about accomplishing during your time here?

When was the last time you considered leaving your job and what was the reason you thought about it?

Preconception: The younger generation waits to be told what to do. They do not take initiative.

Many members of the younger generation have had a more structured upbringing than older generations. Younger people do want to feel they have a 'partner' or a 'go-to person' in the workplace.

Give younger employees a mentor

According to a Deloitte study, Millennials who are at their current job or organization for longer than five years are two times more likely to have a mentor. And according to Price Waterhouse Cooper, 98% of Millennials feel that working with strong mentors is very important.

We often think of a mentor as someone from our personal life: a coach, a teacher, or a community leader. Today, younger people are looking for mentorship in the workplace. According to a study by Springtide Research Institute, over 70% of Generation Z are motivated to go above and beyond when they feel their employer cares about their

---

[3] Stay Interview Questions, https://www.shrm.org/resourcesandtools/tools-and-samples/hr-forms/pages/stayinterviewquestions.aspx

welfare.[4] Having a mentor helps young people feel like you care. Also, greater than 80% want to work for someone with whom they can relate both professionally and personally.

Preconception: Younger generations expect work-life balance on day one of the job.

That is fairly accurate! The younger generations do place a high priority on work-life balance. The key word, however, is balance. They do not expect to be able to ignore their professional duties for their own personal exploits.

WLB (Work-Life Balance)

Young people want and expect a healthy balance between work and personal time. This does not mean they do not love their jobs. Here are four steps to take to ensure everyone in your organization is experiencing WLB equilibrium:

Family Related Benefits:

50% of Millennials have children. They want benefits like childcare providers and paid parental leave.

Holistic Wellness Initiatives:

Help your young professionals with stress management. Offer wearable devices (i.e. fitness watches), mental health support and accessible healthy food options. (This also ties into the Gen Z desire to work for someone who cares about them.)

---

[4] Deichler Andrew, Generation Z Seeks Guidance in the Workplace, https://www.shrm.org/resourcesandtools/hr-topics/organizational-and-employee-development/pages/generation-z-seeks-guidance-in-the-workplace.aspx, 6/28/21

Tuition Reimbursement:

Younger generations have more student debt than previous generations. Additionally, they are experiencing higher levels of financial stress than older generations. Even partial assistance is a great stress reliever to someone who is just beginning their career.

Guaranteed Day Off:

The knowledge that there is one day that is a guaranteed day off makes the long working days doable.

It can be difficult to change our methods or challenge 'the way we have always done it'. I encourage everyone to embrace the younger generations and appreciate the opportunities they bring to your life. At the end of the day, young and seasoned generations all want the same thing: to contribute, make a difference and leave this place better than when they found it.

Immigration

Juanita Duque Serrano

Juanita Duque Serrano was born in Bogotá, Colombia and migrated to the United States at the age of twelve. She holds a Master of Arts degree in Latin American Studies with a focus on crime, law and government from the University of Florida.

In my 7th grade reading class, we read a story about an immigrant girl struggling to make this new country her home. Here I will call her Amira, because after days of searching I have not been able to find the original story. Amira tried to make a home out of a place where no one could pronounce her name, nor did they bother to try. A home where no one could understand her and where they made a point of mentioning her 'strange accent'. The desire to fit in made young Amira embarrassed that her family stood out, and she cringed when there were school events where her family had to be present.

My teacher, Mrs Justice, explained that the lesson of the story was that we should all be proud of ourselves and our families because we are all unique. But her lesson ignored the systemic issues that made this immigrant girl, Amira, feel the way she did. Her lesson placed the blame for all these feelings on the immigrant girl who 'lacked' self-esteem and self-love, rather than on the prevalence of a racial hierarchy that made her feel like she didn't belong, like her accent was out of place, like her family wasn't white enough.

To some, the story might have felt empowering, portraying the notion that if only immigrants had more self-confidence, their immigration experience would be easier. But I felt targeted by the story and scorned by the lesson. I felt all those things that Amira felt. It was as if a spotlight shone bright over me and highlighted a certain guilt. Guilt for being embarrassed. Guilt for being ashamed of the way I spoke. Guilt for not being brave enough to stand up for myself. But what support did I have to do any of those things? There certainly was none in this particular classroom, nor throughout any of my public school education. It wasn't until I was in graduate school, twelve years after I read Amira's story, that I found a support system: a community in the amazing people that flowed through and made up the Latin American Studies Department. I could finally begin to heal! Heal Amira's wounds and my own. I could begin to feel comfortable taking up space and speaking my mind. I found a place where I could learn about the systems built to exclude and separate us and, more importantly, about the people giving their all to tear down these systems. But I want to point out that having access to graduate-level education is a privilege; the United States Department of Education calculates that 40% of immigrant youth do not graduate high school. The system is indeed broken, or is it working just as it was designed?

Immigration is something that all countries deal with, either through the drain of their population or the influx of a new one, sometimes both. Whatever preconceptions you may have, I challenge you to try to imagine a world in which you are the one forced to migrate. Forced to leave loved ones behind. Forced to head for the unknown, where everything you *are* will be unknown.

Of all the many preconceptions that exist regarding immigration, perhaps the greatest one is that our present system of borders and boundaries, on which immigration is predicated, has always been the norm. The boundaries that define global interactions today are relatively new in comparison to the history of the human species. They are a part of a settler colonial project maintained through asymmetric power exchanges, and they do not have to define us. Our species, *homo sapiens*, has been around for at least 200,000 years, but colonial existence has not. As a species, we have been successful in surviving *because* of our constant migration and interaction with humans from different genetic and cultural backgrounds (with the exception of imperialism). Diversity is essential for all life! So, thank immigrants for keeping our species healthy and thriving; our cities alive; food on our tables; personnel in our hospitals; innovation in our universities; for caring for those most valuable in our societies, our children and our elders; fighting for our human rights, and for so much more.

Animals

The Pet Paradox
Primate Art
Dinosaurs
Veganism

The Pet Paradox

Hal Herzog

Hal Herzog is Emeritus Professor of Psychology at Western Carolina University. He has been investigating the complexities of human–animal interactions for over 30 years and is the author of the book Some We Love, Some We Hate, Some We Eat: Why It's So Hard to Think Straight About Animals.

For much of my life, I strongly believed that most of human behavior was determined by our genes. However, my research into pet-keeping, and particularly the complicated relationship we have with dogs, has led me to believe that *cultural* evolution plays a much more dominant force than *biological* evolution in human-animal relations.

Let us look at our relationship with dogs. In many parts of the world and at different points in history, it was considered completely natural to eat dogs. People might have kept them around, but if they got hungry in the cold Arctic, for example, they wouldn't hesitate to grab a puppy and throw it in the stew pot. In other cultures, however, one would never eat a dog. But people decide *not* to consume dogs for different reasons. In the West, we don't eat dogs because we view them as cute and cuddly and members of our families. But in some societies they are not eaten because they are considered unclean and vermin-like. Eating a dog in parts of the Middle East and India would be akin to Westerners eating a rat. Thus, even the reasons why we don't eat creatures such as dogs are culturally dependent and variable.

If you'd asked me about the ethics of pet ownership a few years ago, I would have said everybody gains from the relationship, both the pet owner and the pet. But, recently, it has become harder for me to justify pet ownership. One of the things we have learned from the recent explosion of new research into canines and newer developments in cognitive anthropology is that certain dogs have mental capacities that we never would have imagined them to have ten to fifteen years ago. Research suggests that dogs can read human emotions fairly accurately, in the same way humans can pick up on others' feelings. Research aside, if you ask most people what they actually think, they would endorse the notion that dogs do have human-like emotions.

The problem is that while we have increasingly recognized pets' agency as beings, at the same time we continue to treat them as property. At the average pet store, the first thing we do with our dogs is cut their testicles off. When people say, "My pet's a member of the family," would you cut the testicles off one of your own kids? Yet that is exactly what we do with our pets. We've also played God in other ways that have been detrimental to dogs. Take the French Bulldog that many find so adorable. In our breeding efforts to produce those flat wrinkly faces with shortened nostrils that make them so cute, we have created a dog that is prone to respiratory and cardiac problems, skin disorders and other genetic diseases. In many ways, we have inflicted serious harm to the canine genome as we have bred them to have weird human-like physical traits. The ultimate paradox is that the more we recognize pets as individuals with personalities, thoughts and desires, the less moral it is to keep them as pets.

Don't get me wrong; I am a pet lover myself, and I will continue to keep having pets. But why do we do it? Why do *I* do it? We keep animals as pets for the same reason that I eat meat. I eat meat because it tastes good. I know the arguments against meat consumption, and I actually agree with them. Yet, like 95% of Americans, I still eat meat; it brings me pleasure. The justification for bringing pets into our lives is essentially the same as my morally bankrupt justification for eating animals—they bring us pleasure. The sociologist Leslie Irvine compares the practice of pet-keeping with slavery. Part of me thinks she is right.

So, what to make of all this? There are two branches of ethics. Prescriptive ethics is a realm of philosophy that tells people what they *ought* to do. Descriptive ethics, in contrast, is the realm of psychology that studies what people are *actually* doing. My research on human-animal interactions is in the latter camp. I am not in the business of telling people what to do.

But if there is any advice I can offer, it is the following. We only go around once in this life. Our interactions with animals, such as meat eating and pet keeping, raise fascinating and important issues. But, at some point, we should acknowledge our inconsistencies and learn to live with them. Complete moral consistency can be a heavy burden. The moral high ground has its advantages, but on the other hand, living with paradox is part of the human condition.

Primate Art

Charmaine Quinn

Charmaine Quinn is known as the muse for famed capuchin monkey abstract expressionist artist Pockets Warhol. Charmaine has volunteered for many years with rescued orangutans in Borneo as well as howler monkeys in Belize and Story Book Farm Primate Sanctuary. Charmaine feels deeply about issues involving animal welfare and the illegal exotic animal trade.

I have been fascinated with primate art since the moment I realized that these interesting creatures share a gift for creativity with humans. It is slightly perplexing to think of non-human primates as artists, but in fact there are many of these undiscovered and talented artists capable of creative intent.

Since we are all from the primate family and capable of high intellect, it is not surprising that they are able to produce such beautiful abstract pieces of art. Just as some humans are motivated to paint or draw, so are some chimpanzees, orangutans, gorillas and monkeys, as well as many other animals.

Many of these artists are able to express themselves in sanctuary settings when given the proper tools. I have had the privilege of volunteering in Borneo with orangutans, where I was able to observe their cognition in the form of problem solving. Witnessing orangutan art projects at a conference for primates aroused my curiosity.

I currently volunteer at Story Book Farm Primate Sanctuary with a rescued capuchin monkey who has become world famous as an abstract painter (Pockets Warhol) after I introduced him to non-toxic paints ten years ago. At the time of his arrival, I noticed some physical characteristics that reminded me of Andy Warhol and attached the Warhol name to Pockets. I continue weekly with his regular painting sessions, where he uses a variety of colours to create a diverse collection of interesting pieces.

Pockets has become something of a 'celebrity' over the past decade. He has painted hundreds of canvases, which have both traveled across the world and been published in *National Geographic Learning*, *MacLeans*, *Rolling Stone* and *Variety*. He was the subject of a Canadian Broadcasting Commission short documentary film, *Portrait of Pockets,* and his artwork has even been recognized by his namesake, the Warhol Museum. His paintings are sold to raise funds for the sanctuary, and I often donate his paintings to help other animal charities in their efforts to raise funds and awareness. Pockets' paintings are in the hands of many fascinating humans in arts, conservation, science and animal welfare, including Dame Jane Goodall, Col. Chris Hadfield, Ricky Gervais and Jann Arden, just to name a few.

While Pockets has the best life he possibly can in a sanctuary, his life should truly be in the forest of South America with a monkey troop of his own. Due to the exotic animal trade and human intervention, his life has gone down a different path. It is important that people are aware that non-human primates are sentient beings and deserving of a life in the wild where they were meant to be. Pockets' art has helped illuminate the scope of animal intelligence to the mainstream. It is impossible to look at his artwork and not feel *something*. His paintings remind us that art is not unique to humans and, more importantly, neither are the qualities of creativity, emotion, and higher-level thinking.

My hope is that Pockets, fondly known as the 'Warhol Monkey', can help people re-appreciate our similarities with other animals and deepen our connection with all sentient beings.

Dinosaurs

Kallie Moore

Kallie Moore manages the University of Montana Paleontology Collection and is a host on PBS Eons, *a YouTube channel dedicated to the history of life on Earth.*

As humans, it can be tough to comprehend the billions of years that preceded our existence. All we have ever known is a world completely and, in many respects overly, dominated by our own species, *Homo sapiens*. Aside from the earth's 'human-less' *past*, it can be equally challenging for humans to consider a *future* devoid of *Homo sapiens* as the dominant species.

As a paleontologist, I am immersed daily in the records and fossils of the past, particularly those of dinosaurs. It never ceases to amaze me how a creature of such size and magnitude that once dominated the world for so many years could essentially just disappear. Let me try and shed some light on the scope of just how dominant dinosaurs once were in this world.

In terms of size, some of them were the largest land animals that ever existed, over a hundred feet long and up to seventy tons. You could think of some of them as walking blue whales! There's simply nothing like them today.

In terms of their time on Earth, dinosaurs were around for approximately 175 million years. Contrast that to the mere 300,000 years that *Homo sapiens* has been around, and their longevity is almost impossible to grasp. Dinosaurs first show up in the fossil record in the late Triassic Period, about 240 million years ago. At this point in time, dinosaurs only comprised about 6-10% of animals in any ecosystem. It wasn't until the Jurassic Period when dinosaurs really took off. Just ten million years into the Jurassic Period, they were far and away the most dominant land animal on Earth, having spread everywhere across the globe.

Dinosaurs existed for such a long span that many of the most well-known dinosaurs didn't even overlap together in their time on earth. *Stegosaurus*, for example, lived in the late Jurassic Period, about 155 million years ago, whereas *T. rex* existed about 67 million years ago. Thus, *T. rex* actually lived closer in time to humans than it did to *Stegosaurus*!

The point is, dinosaurs ruled this world for a very, very, very long time, with a dominance that is tough for the human mind to fully comprehend. Yet, despite such dominance, the reign of the dinosaurs *did* come to an end, when a giant seven- to ten-mile-wide asteroid slammed into the earth over 66 million years ago. The sheer impact of the asteroid, the subsequent release of radioactive dust into the air, and concurrent volcanic eruptions formed a lethal combination that was able to wipe out the dinosaurs in a very short period of time, probably within one generation.

Perhaps my biggest takeaway from the dinosaurs is that even if you're the dominant form of life for 175 million years, your day will end, one way or another. For the dinosaurs, it ended with a giant space rock. For humans, perhaps it will end with climate change, or some other supernatural event. But just like the day of the dinosaurs came to an end, so will the day of *Homo sapiens*. That's probably the best knowledge that the dinosaurs have imparted to us.

As a paleontologist, I feel like the history, and particularly the extinction, of the dinosaurs, has given me a much deeper respect for everything that is alive today. Knowing that our time is limited and knowing that species are only on this planet for a very short period of time makes everything in life feel more weighted. Whole lineages can disappear in the blink of an eye. And they can't come back. Extinction is final.

Humans are currently towing the line of extinction. And, while the dinosaurs showed us that all lineages do die out at some point, knowing that *we* may be the cause of our own demise is a tough pill to swallow. I think if more people understood how finite extinctions were, they might respect nature and our earth a little bit more.

Veganism

Corey Wrenn, PhD

Dr Corey Wrenn is lecturer of sociology with the School of Social Policy, Sociology and Social Research (SSPSSR) and co-director of the Centre for the Study of Social and Political Movements at the University of Kent, United Kingdom. She served as chair of the American Sociological Association's Animals and Society section and co-founded the International Association of Vegan Sociologists in 2020. She is book review editor for Society and Animals, *editor for* The Sociological Quarterly, *a member of The Vegan Society's Research Advisory Committee, and hosts the* Sociology and Animals *podcast. In July 2013, she founded the Vegan Feminist Network, an academic-activist project engaging intersectional social justice praxis. She is the author of* A Rational Approach to Animal Rights: Extensions in Abolitionist Theory *(2016),* Piecemeal Protest: Animal Rights in the Age of Nonprofits *(2019), and* Animals in Irish Society *(2021).*

It's common for many to view the veganism movement as 'extreme'. The idea of swearing away not only meat, but *all* animal products in general, can seem like an over-reaction, a notion so divorced from our daily lives that it can be easily deemed extremist. But to me, it's actually quite mind-boggling that I would be considered extreme for being a vegan.

Veganism is only extreme when you view it through the preconceived lens of the status quo, a status quo that dictates that it is 'normal' to kill and eat non-human animals and to abuse them for the purpose of deriving their eggs, milk and other products. Let me tell you what *I* consider extreme—drinking breastmilk from another animal. We routinely take and drink the breastmilk from another species. It's not even the milk of an ape, but the milk of a bovine. We take the breastmilk of a completely different species that is meant for a calf! We then take that milk, put sugar in it, make milkshakes, freeze it and make ice cream, and consume it in a variety of ways. *That* feels extreme.

Another very 'normal' practice that I consider extreme is the act of eating a hamburger. What can be more extreme than saying, "I fancy a hamburger today, so let's go stick a bolt gun into this animal's brain so we can chop them up and eat them." Nothing is more extreme than when we feel it's totally acceptable to kill other sentient beings that share our own capacity for love, friendship, suffering, pain and fear. Just like us, they don't want to die; they yearn to survive, and they fear death. Yet we feel like we can do whatever we want to them, just because their bodies taste good, or their breastmilk tastes good.

What often gets forgotten is that for most of human history, humans actually ate a plant-based diet. That was the norm for a very long time in our 300,000 years of existence. In the grand scope of human history, our present animal-eating culture is actually a very small blip. The hunter-gatherer phenomenon is only a recent economy that human societies have developed. Before that, humans were mostly gatherers, and they were mostly vegetarians. They scavenged whatever they could eat, and the archaeology is clear that their diet was mostly plant-based.

When the landscape shifted about 10,000 years ago, hunting became a little easier and more realistic, albeit still extremely dangerous. People were still quite heavily living off plants, berries, fungi, and vegetarian foods. It wasn't until the dawn of agricultural societies that it became 'normal' to domesticate other animals. And such domestication coincided with this philosophy that it was okay to completely dominate another species for the purposes of convenience, profit, and a variety of other reasons.

We have this tendency to think that anything that deviates substantially from our present-day norms is extreme. And anything deemed extreme is subsequently viewed in a negative light. But I would encourage people to think outside the status quo. Just because something has become normalized by the masses doesn't mean it is right. And often, if you look back in history, you will realize that our present-day status quo is actually quite different from the norms of the past. Thousands of years ago, it would have seemed extreme to eat and manufacture meat and animal products in the way we do now. So how extreme can veganism truly be viewed today, when being vegan was a core of humanity for so much of our past?

Parenthood

Infertility
The Baby Decision
Regretting Motherhood

Infertility

Dr Kimberly Liu

Kimberly Liu is a gynecologic reproductive endocrinology and infertility specialist in Toronto. She is currently the medical director of Mount Sinai Fertility and an associate professor at the University of Toronto.

As an obstetrician who specializes in infertility, I work with many couples who experience challenges in conceiving. With modern advances in reproductive endocrinology, I am fortunate that my efforts to help many of these couples are much more successful than they would have been even just a decade ago.

In our efforts to help curb infertility, however, what can often get lost is how challenging it can be to conceive in the first place. The preconception in society is that it is totally *normal* for humans to reproduce successfully. The expectation is that any challenges in reproduction are abnormal. In reality, though, when you consider all the biological processes that need to line up in order for a pregnancy to occur, becoming pregnant is actually quite challenging. Even under ideal circumstances, the chances for conception are about 10-20% per month. In fact, when I think about all the factors that must align for a successfully pregnancy, I often find myself marvelling at how much of a *miracle* it is every time a pregnancy *does* occur.

The following is a brief overview of the circumstances and sequence of events that need to happen for a pregnancy to occur.

Unlike men, who can continue to produce more sperm throughout their life, women are born with a specific number of eggs. As a woman progresses through her lifetime, the number of eggs declines. In fact, women actually lose most of their eggs before they are even born. Between the time a female is conceived until she is born, her egg count declines from approximately twenty million to one million eggs. Then, by the time a female reaches puberty and ovulation starts to occur, further eggs have been lost, and she only has about half a million eggs left.

During a normal menstrual cycle, one egg will be released each month. Over the course of a lifespan, most women probably release somewhere between 300 and 500 eggs. This number varies based on many factors, including how many pregnancies the woman has had and use of contraception.

The process of losing eggs is an ongoing one, where eggs develop and then, on their own, they become atretic, which means that they naturally die off. Eggs are constantly dying off via this natural process. That is the mechanism by which women lose most of their eggs over their lifetime. By the time a woman reaches menopause, very few eggs are left.

In addition to reduced egg quantity, there is also the matter of egg quality. When addressing egg quality, we are referring to the genetics of the egg itself, and the factors within the egg that determine whether it is likely to grow and become fertilized to become a healthy embryo. With age, the genetics of an egg can deteriorate. Recall that these eggs have been present in the body since even before the woman was born and have thus been subject to all sorts of potential environmental factors that are cumulative over time.

By the time a woman is thirty-five, probably only about 50% of a woman's eggs would be normal, and 50% would be abnormal. That number of normal eggs continues to decline dramatically. By the time a woman turns forty, there may only be 20% of her eggs that are still normal. By the time a woman turns forty-five, only about 1% of her eggs are normal.

If we look at the thirty-five-year-old woman with approximately only 50% of her eggs considered normal, that means there is only a 50% chance each month that she is releasing a viable egg that could even potentially be compatible with fertility. Then, assuming the egg is normal, we of course need to take the sperm into account.

The sperm needs to be in the reproductive tract at the right time. Sperm only lasts for a few days, and it needs to be present right before the time of ovulation. A couple needs to have intercourse at the right time, the sperm must be normal, and it needs to be able to reach the egg through a patent reproductive tract. Finally, assuming both the sperm and egg are normal, the sperm must then enter the egg, at which point it starts to grow and divide into an embryo. These steps are only the beginning of the journey towards a healthy pregnancy and birth.

As one can see, there are many factors that govern the ability to conceive, and many steps that must occur simultaneously for a pregnancy to occur. This brings us back to the preconception that getting pregnant is easy. Humans are actually *not* very effective in the reproductive process, because of the fact that all these factors have to line up at a particular moment in time. Pregnancy truly is a miraculous process!

The Baby Decision

Merle Bombardieri

Merle Bombardieri, MSW, LICSW is the author of the bestselling The Baby Decision: How to Make the Most Important Choice of Your Life *and has contributed to* Our Bodies, Ourselves, *the* Boston Globe, *medical journals and a medical textbook. She is also a psychotherapist in Massachusetts and parenthood decision-making coach. One of the greatest pleasures in her career is remote coaching with people all over the world. Although she is a mother, she has been a child-free advocate since 1978.*

The preconception for anyone considering parenthood:

"You shouldn't have a child unless you're 100% sure."

Are you leaning toward starting a family, but totally terrified about parenthood and the possibility that you will regret your decision? This common misconception inflicts on decision-makers totally unnecessary bitten nails, torn-out hair and, worst of all, sleepless nights.

The preconception for anyone leaning toward remaining childfree:

"You can't call it a decision if you have any positive fantasies of parenthood or if you worry about FOMO."

As an expert on parenthood decision-making, I participate in a Reddit chat group, r/fencesitter, with over 41,000 members. These two preconceptions appear constantly.

The truth is that most people who are now happy parents occasionally, or frequently, doubted their choice before and during pregnancy and/or the adoption process. This includes people who "have always known" they wanted to have a family, and even people who went through fertility treatment or adoption applications.

Although many people make this decision with a partner, for the sake of simplicity, I am going to focus on your individual choice, which you can also discuss with your partner, if you have one.

Use these three ideas to replace the 100% uncertainty myth.

1. Ambivalence is a normal part of being human. Therefore, it is reasonable to expect some doubt and regret about even the right decision. The parenthood decision is the only one you cannot reverse. You can move to a different home or country, get divorced, change jobs or careers. But once you're a parent, you're a parent forever. You'd have to be anesthetized to have zero worries about childbirth, a sick or difficult child, depleted finances, a wrecked love relationship, or the twenty-year obligation. I tell my clients and readers, "60/40 is a decision. When you lean 60% toward a childfree or parenting choice, that's the beginning of a decision." You'll probably wait till you get to 70/30 or 80/20 before calling it a decision. Don't hold your breath waiting for 100%. Not going to happen, and it doesn't have to. Once you know this, you can trust your decision even if it comes with a side of doubt.

These percentages work for childfree decision-makers, too.

2. Every decision involves loss, so doubt, even about a good decision, makes sense. Once you decide, you gain the potential satisfactions offered by your choice, but you also lose the potential satisfactions of the other choice. The word 'decide', as I wrote in my book *The Baby Decision: How to Make the Most Important Choice of Your Life*, comes from a Latin root meaning 'to cut away from'. The existentialist psychotherapist Irwin Yalom said, "For every yes, there must be a no. Decisions are expensive because they cost you everything else."

Choosing parenthood means losing freedom and spontaneity, while choosing to be childfree means giving up the potential joys of family life. Grieving the satisfactions of the other choice may allow you to be more excited about the choice you make. Potential parents may want to plan with a partner or friends for time away from the baby and for exercise and meditation, for instance. Childfree decision-makers may want to plan time with nieces and nephews, volunteer work or mentoring, but only if they have a need to nurture. This isn't true for all childfree people (another preconception!). I call this type of planning 'stealing a little from the other choice'.

3. The right way to decide: Don't ask, "Will I regret my decision?" You probably will, at times. Ask, "Which decision will I regret least?" This will help you trust your choice. If you anticipate some doubt, you can let the decision jell, with at least the beginning of peace of mind.

If you wait to be 100% certain, you will grow old getting a very sore bottom from sitting on the fence. Instead, use your knowledge of ambivalence to jump off that fence and into the joys of your chosen life.

Regretting Motherhood

Orna Donath, PhD

Orna Donath is a doctor of sociology who has studied and teaches in the fields of non-motherhood, motherhood, time, and emotions from sociological and feminist perspectives. She is a social activist and the author of the book Regretting Motherhood, *which was translated into 15 languages. In addition to her academic research, she has served as the chairwoman of the governing board of one of the rape crisis centers in Israel, where she has volunteered since 2004.*

My areas of research are the unwillingness of women to become mothers, and the regret of women who became mothers. It is important here to be clear on what qualifies as 'regret'. I am not speaking of ambivalence. Many mothers might feel ambivalent. They might admit that being a parent is really challenging and causes them suffering and distress sometimes. But at the end of the day, they still resonate with the saying that 'the smile of their child' makes it all worth it for them. This is not what I refer to when I speak of regret. Most of the women I interviewed did not have any ifs, ands, or buts when reflecting on their choice to become mothers.

There were three parameters by which I defined regret in my study. First off, the title of the study was *Regretting Parenthood*. Parents who approached me had read this title and self-identified to some extent with it. Second, each woman was asked: if they could go back in time with the experience and knowledge that they have today, would they still become a mother? Each of the women included in the study said they wouldn't. And third, I asked each woman if they felt there were any advantages to being a mother. Some of the participants said they *did* experience certain advantages, but they were outweighed by the disadvantages, and other mothers expressed that they felt no advantages at all. I make a point of outlining the criteria here to give you a very clear picture of the definition of regret in my study.

We live in a society that does not really give us the permission to regret. We are allowed and expected to regret only if we commit a crime or a sin, but if the act is outside the arenas of religion or the law, we are expected not to regret. Regret is seen as failure. There are books on how to live a 'regret-free life'. But humans *do* regret many things in life—marriages, relationships, career paths, and yes—even becoming a parent. Motherhood, like all human experiences and relationships, does not transcend the possibility of regret. Yet women are told from a young age that motherhood will change their lives. If they express hesitation, they are told it will be different when it is their own child and that being a mother is a role they will grow into, even if it doesn't feel like it now. For some women, becoming a mother is so indoctrinated into the normal path of life that they never even question it, even if it is something they don't necessarily yearn for.

In my opinion, why can't we regret? It's not a shame for me to regret. It's a very human thing to admit we made a mistake; it is part of being a subject. We cannot predict everything in the future. Life is not a linear process, and we do not evolve in a straight line. We are allowed to look back, remember, evaluate, understand that perhaps we didn't make the best decision, and sometimes even lament about it. There's a saying, 'Don't cry over spilled milk', about which I ask two questions. First, why can't we cry? It's okay to cry. We don't have to be happy all the time; that is part of life and the human experience. And the second question—who spilled the milk from the outset? What I try to show in my research is that the hands that spilled the milk are not necessarily the personal hands of the women. Women are told by society that motherhood is a certain 'need' shared by all those who are defined as 'female', and that is misleading, a partial truth. Yes—for many women, it will change their lives for the better. But that doesn't mean it will be the case for all of us.

I do the work I do with the hope of reducing suffering. I think that talking to each other honestly, listening without judgment, and having the freedom to express how we truly feel might expand our liberties and depth of understanding. We must talk about the way we are pushed into motherhood sometimes. Without a complex public-personal discussion, it might be devastating for women. It might be devastating for men. It might be devastating for children. And the only way to truly have that conversation is by first *acknowledging* that such regret does indeed exist. That is why I continue to do the work that I do.

Historical Figures

A Jewish Jesus
Napoleon
Karl Marx

A Jewish Jesus

Eric M Meyers, PhD

Eric M Meyers is the Bernice and Morton Lerner Emeritus Professor of Religious and Jewish Studies at Duke University. He founded the Center for Jewish Studies at Duke in 1972. His specialties include biblical studies and archaeology. He has directed or co-directed digs in Israel and Italy for over forty years and has authored hundreds of articles, reviews, reports and 15 books. Together with his wife, Carol Meyers, he co-authored commentaries on Haggai and Zechariah in the Anchor Bible Series. He served as editor-in-chief of The Oxford Encyclopedia of Archaeology in the Near East *(1997). His most recent excavations at Sepphoris were fully published in 2018 by Penn State University Press under the Eisenbrauns imprint. He also served for three terms as President of ASOR (The American Schools/Society of Overseas Research).*

One of the least well understood facts about Jesus among Christians is that in his life he was fully Jewish; Christianity arose only many years later, most notably after it spread west to Europe following the Destruction of the Temple in Jerusalem in 70 CE. For Jews, not appreciating one of the greatest teachers in their own tradition or knowing very little about him is a serious hindrance to better understanding most of their neighbors in an era of multi-culturalism. And I'm sorry to say most Jews don't really care or are quite negative on the subject. As for the Christian community in all its diversity, many still remain uninformed or disinterested in the fact that Judaism and early Christianity were so interconnected in their most formative period in the Land of Israel, the First Century.

Despite these attitudes, the past twenty years or so has witnessed a sea change in the amount of information gained through archaeology leading to a reassessment of the early life of Jesus of Nazareth. Until then the two competing views of Jesus were these: 1. Jesus was a Greek speaker and a kind of philosopher who reached out to the broader public, fully participating in the emerging Greco-Roman culture that surrounded him in Galilee; 2. Jesus was a commoner from a more or less illiterate Jewish population in Galilee who attracted a large following due to his charismatic personality, and his language was Aramaic.

My own archaeological field work during this period was at Sepphoris, just 4 km from Nazareth as the crow flies. Herod Antipas, son of Herod the Great, was making it into 'the ornament of all Galilee' as its new capitol during Jesus' early years. But what we found in our first century layers on the western summit were large houses with ritual baths in them, thirty in all, with many fragments of chalk-stone vessels that are impervious to ritual impurity defilement.

Alongside these obvious markers of Jewish identity and Torah observance, no remains whatsoever of pork consumption emerged in our faunal assemblage. As for evidence of Greek culture, there simply was none.

In dig after dig across Galilee, the same pattern was found in small villages and towns as well as in the larger cities such as Sepphoris, Tiberius and Magdala/Tarichaea. There is virtually no evidence of gentile life in the hundreds of known sites and ample support for a Jewish community that was observant in biblical laws of purity and dietary restrictions. And to this growing trove of data we now have many Galilean synagogues from the time of Jesus as well, including two from the seaside Galilean town of Magdala, just north of Tiberias on the western shore of the Sea of Galilee. Others are Gamla in the Golan,

Mt. Tabor, Capernaum, and Cana. In other words, the myth of a gentile Galilee has been exposed and destroyed, and the evidence now shows that Galilee was overwhelmingly Jewish and was not yet Hellenized. Greek culture is nowhere to be found in the time of Jesus. So why was Jesus rejected from the synagogue in Nazareth (Mark 6:1-6; Matt 13:54-58; Luke 4:16-30)? In my view, the relocation of the royal family to Sepphoris and the extensive building going on there, with all their retinue and baggage (killing of John the Baptist), did not sit well with Jesus, whose focus was on the poor. Seeing his fellow villagers rush there to cash in on the building boom was too much, hence tensions were high when he visited his home town.

The picture of Jesus that emerges after all the new work of recent years is that of a dedicated master teacher who was familiar with the Torah and concentrated his efforts on addressing the largely agricultural inhabitants and fishermen of Galilee and the Lake region; as a result, his most favored town was Capernaum, from whence he went out into 'all Galilee'. While focusing on the poor and mostly illiterate class, it is clear from the New Testament that the multitudes were not ignorant of the Hebrew Bible and its stories and were accustomed to obeying many of its laws, especially the Sabbath, purity and dietary laws. This meant they were attuned aurally to learning and when Jesus came to preach and teach them, he picked from the tradition some of the best vignettes and nuggets from Psalms, Isaiah and the prophets. But when he was asked what the greatest commandment was, he answered as follows in Matthew 22: 37-40: verse 37: "You shall love the Lord your God with all your heart, and with all your soul, and with all your mind." (Deuteronomy 6:5) "And Jesus added this: This is the greatest and first commandment. (v 37) And a second is like it: you shall love your neighbor as yourself. (Levitical 19:18) On these two commandments hang all the law and the prophets." The first commandment is the beginning of the Shema prayer central to all Jewish liturgy, and the second of course is the Golden Rule, the undergirding of all interfaith activity and the inspiration for the noble idea of welcoming the stranger.

In short, it should be perfectly clear how the original followers of Jesus were observant Jews, familiar no doubt with large portions of the Hebrew Bible and largely from small towns and villages in Galilee. The parting of the ways came much later, but certainly this common beginning links the two communities inextricably. Only by accepting this common origin and learning about it can Jews and Christians come closer together and remove the stain of prejudice and persecution from our troubled past.

Napoleon

Andrew Roberts

Andrew Roberts is a British historian and internationally acclaimed author of the books The Storm of War, Churchill: Walking with Destiny, Napoleon the Great, *and* George III: The Life and Reign of Britain's Most Misunderstood Monarch.

Napoleon Bonaparte died just over 200 years ago, but his legacy finds itself at a unique juncture in history. On the one hand, there is of course nobody alive today who ever met him who can provide a personal account. Yet by the same token, he is not so remote a figure as Julius Caesar or Alexander the Great, where the legacy is established and essentially set in stone.

While doing the research for my book, *Napoleon the Great*, I read over 38,000 of Napoleon's personal letters, spanning from his childhood up until just a couple of weeks before his death. This provided me with deep insights into many facets of his life with regard to his personality, military achievement, leadership style and motivations. As his legacy becomes more intransient with the passage of time, I can comment on several of the preconceptions that have come to define the historical figure of Napoleon. In the following vignette, I shall share several insights on a few of the preconceptions that tend to predominate popular thought.

The preconception: Napoleon was just a military conqueror.

Yes, Napoleon was an extremely impressive military general. Of the 60 battles he fought, he won a stunning 47 of them; quite an incredible record. What is perhaps more remarkable is that he was able to win battles of all sorts, whether he had more or fewer men than the enemy, more or less cavalry than the enemy, or more or less cannon than the enemy. He could win whether he was retreating or advancing, whether he was concentrating on the right or left flank, and whether he was relieving a garrison from a city or breaking out of one. The sheer dexterity and multiplicity of the situations in which he managed to find victory were truly extraordinary. And, of course, the sheer magnitude of his military conquests was so extensive that one would have to go back to Alexander the Great, Julius Caesar or Hannibal to witness anything like it. He fought in battlefields spanning sixteen countries.

But in the shadow of these impressive military accomplishments, what can sometimes get lost is the man behind the general. Napoleon was a reformer. He believed in equality before the law, freedom to worship, and the concept of meritocracy—modern principles that many societies live by today, but which were considered revolutionary back in France in the late 18th and early 19th centuries. And his reforming sweep didn't stop at the borders of France; The Napoleonic code formed the basis of government in the Rhineland in Germany until the year 1900, and traces can still be found in the legal codes of many countries even today, including the United States. This doesn't mean his reforms were positive for everyone; his policies were intensely sexist and placed the males of the family in an immensely powerful position. Nonetheless, he was a significant reformer of his time and sought to spread these liberal ideologies across Europe.

On a personal level, Napoleon was also an intellectual. He was an avid reader and studied philosophy. He even wrote short stories and a couple of novellas, some of which are still in circulation in bookshops 200 years later. He was a very complex man who thought deeply.

The preconception: Napoleon was a prototype for the 20th century dictator.

One of the points I try to emphasize in my book is that Napoleon wasn't just some kind of maniac who invaded countries for the sheer heck of it. Of the seven Coalition Wars, or Napoleonic Wars, only two were started by Napoleon. The other five wars were waged by his enemies against him, either invading or attacking France or her allies. Thus, the majority of his wars were fighting on the defensive. Further, the two wars that he *did* wage were not motivated by conquering more land but were rather driven by economic reasons.

Yes—Napoleon did establish a dictatorship and, after a referendum, declared himself emperor for life. But it's very important to understand that the concept of dictatorship in France was wholly removed from the kind of murderous antisemitic dictatorships that emerged in the 20th century. He was not a totalitarian dictator. He had no large-scale police, he had no antisemitic beliefs, and he had no desire to rule the minds of all his subjects in the way one later sees in the 20th century dictators.

This is not to say he was totally benevolent. He did commit two atrocities in particular, which would be considered war crimes in the modern sense. In Padua in 1796, he put down a revolt of the Italian Catholic Church with untoward aggression. And, more infamously, in 1799, he executed an estimated 3,000 Turkish artillerymen in Jaffa. Yet in the case of Jaffa, the Turks had given their parole, meaning they had promised not to raise up arms against the French republic when they had been captured in the Gaza area six weeks earlier. When they were then re-captured, however, having fought against the French Republic at the siege of Jaffa, he had them executed. That is clearly a war crime in the modern sense, but at the time, if you broke your parole in the eighteenth century in this part of the world, you did forfeit your life. This is not to excuse the atrocities that Napoleon committed, but it is also a far stretch to compare his atrocities to anything close to the

Holocaust, the mass starvation of Ukrainians, or the murder of 60 million people in China by Mao. I think these are an entirely different set of atrocities and it would be a mistake to associate Napoleon with any of the brutal totalitarian dictators who emerged in the 20th century.

The preconception: The Napoleon Complex

I'm sure there is such thing as a Napoleon complex … it's just that Napoleon didn't have one. He had no feelings of inferiority. All this business of him being short is complete rubbish. He was 5'5, which was actually the average height of a Frenchman in the 18th century. The reason people thought he was so small was that British caricaturists constantly made him look small in an attempt to denigrate him. But, in reality, he was of average size.

He also didn't have the hubristic aspect of the Napoleon complex, where one is uber aggressive and overconfident. Some might point to his failed invasion in Russia as an act of hubris, but at the time, he had already beaten Russia twice, and when he set off on his failed 1812 campaign, he had no intention of spending more than three weeks in Russia. It was other circumstances that later developed in the war that led to the disaster that ensued.

Napoleon was a fascinating man. My book has hopefully shed light on the truth of who he was: his strengths, his flaws and his complexities. As time continues to pass and we get further away from the period of his life, my hope is that some of the preconceptions in popular culture about this intriguing figure can be replaced by the truer reality of who he was, what he did and what he stood for.

Karl Marx

Terrell Carver

Terrell Carver is Professor of Political Theory at The University of Bristol, UK.

Karl Marx has somehow generated the world's largest array of preconceptions, starting after his death in 1883. This 'legacy' is possibly a rival to the 2000-year history of Christian apologetics on the teachings of Jesus.

During his lifetime Marx was very little known, had even less fame, and wrote a very, very large number of words now published in some hundreds of volumes. Almost all this material was unpublished in his lifetime.

Most of the material that was published when he was alive appeared in newspapers. For most of those papers he was an editorial-writer or foreign correspondent, so, by definition, his writing was topical and ephemeral. He saw only one substantial book through the press, and otherwise his métier was the paper-bound political pamphlet.

However, this is not what you'll read in the general run of biographies, whether admiring, hostile or sardonic. That about sums up his reception since the graveside encomium given by his friend and literary executor Friedrich Engels.

Engels's published appreciation set the tone and template: Marx was a great thinker and great revolutionary, the equal of Hegel in philosophy and Darwin in science, a master of theory and method, an inspiring leader but self-effacing guru.

Marx's own rare ventures into self-explanation—only a very few lines dashed off in a preface and an afterword—alerted readers to his 'view', his 'outlook', his 'conception', as he put it.

Others turned those rather tentative clues to his originality into 'the materialist interpretation of history', 'scientific socialism', and the eponymous 'Marxism'—notwithstanding his reported remark (in French) that he was "not a Marxist."

Thus, in the biographies and commentaries we're taken through Karl's earliest years, teleologically. So, we follow his 'journey' along a path that everybody now knows was how this rather wild-eyed youth got to be 'Marx'.

It's a short step from that hindsight to the twentieth-century iconography of the grey-beards—Marx and his sidekick as wise old men. For millions of followers and a few famous leaders, all on journeys of their own during the decades after his death, the image was the message.

What exactly was the message was something for scholars to puzzle over. But along the way quite a lot was forgotten or erased, de-selected and deleted. Alternatively, some things were bigged-up, mythologized and misconstrued.

In his lifetime, and as an actual living person, Marx was a political activist, openly scornful of philosophers, philosophizing, and philosophy. His political extremism was lodged in democratic politics, which was revolutionary at the time by definition. Thus, to the authoritarian and obscurantist regimes that he was resisting, he was himself seditious and treasonous.

Marx's epiphany came during the revolutionary events that swept across the European continent in 1848-1849, when the first national elections were held under universal (male) suffrage. Constitutional assemblies convened themselves, democratic governments were launched, and the 'crowned heads of Europe' fled to save their necks.

After the anti-democratic repressions and reactionary restorations, Marx retreated to his study, necessarily and regretfully. As a political exile, he lived quite a marginal existence on the poverty-line in insalubrious London, blaming himself for the hardships he had inflicted on his family. As an undocumented non-citizen of nowhere, he had to mind his 'Ps & Qs'. In his native Rhenish Prussia, he had been tried *in absentia* as a traitor.

You'll find factual traces of the above in the many, many biographies that have accumulated over the years. But, armed with the above, you'll be in a good position to check out the wonderful world of preconceptions, and you'll see just how the great 'Marx' has been preconceived.

Crime

On Death Row
In Prison for Murder
Indigenous Injustice

On Death Row

James Acker

James Acker is a Distinguished Teaching Professor Emeritus in the School of Criminal Justice at the University at Albany. His scholarship includes several books and articles addressing capital punishment.

Assume that a man (98% of the more than 2,400 individuals currently awaiting execution in the United States are men) has been convicted of capital murder and, following a hearing to determine whether he will spend the rest of his life in prison or instead be sentenced to death, he stands before a judge who solemnly pronounces that he will die by lethal injection. A hush falls over the courtroom. Two armed law enforcement officers handcuff him and escort him from the room. The door closes behind them. What happens next might surprise you. When the sentence of death has been passed, the preconception might be that death is the only punishment served. In reality, though, the death sentence is just the beginning of a long and arduous road, one on which that man will spend years in some of the worst conditions imaginable.

Not surprisingly, rounds of appeals will follow to enable higher courts to determine whether errors were committed that require a new trial or at least a new sentencing hearing. This will take some time. How much time may be surprising. Between 2016 and 2020, the last five years for which information is available, an average of 19.6 years lapsed between an offender's capital sentencing and his execution (Snell,

2021: 17, Table 12). The average time that other prisoners now under sentence of death have spent behind bars is roughly the same: 19.4 years (Snell, 2021: 2). Many have been awaiting execution more than three decades (Death Penalty Information Center, n.d.a), while Raymond Riles spent 45 years on Texas' death row before he was re-sentenced to life imprisonment (Lozano, 2021). Why do appeals take so long?

Death-penalty trials are long and complicated. Because human life is on the line, cases undergo multiple layers of judicial review, first in the state courts (assuming the crime was not prosecuted by the federal government or US Military) in one of the 27 states that currently authorize capital punishment, and then in the federal courts. Reversals are not uncommon; indeed, they are considerably more likely than an execution. Roughly 16% to 25% of the more than 8,000 death sentences imposed since 1973 will end with an execution. In the remaining cases, individuals will have their capital conviction or sentence reversed if they do not first die of natural causes (Baumgartner *et al.*, 2018: 139-155; Liebman, Fagan & West, 2000). An alarming number of individuals—186 through 2021—have been released from death row after being exonerated, including 29 following the results of DNA analysis (Death Penalty Information Center, n.d.b). Researchers have estimated that 4.1%—or one in 25—of all persons sentenced to death in the US since 1973 are innocent (Gross *et al.*, 2014).

Under what conditions are the men and women who have been sentenced to death confined? In most jurisdictions, they are relegated to death row housing, where they are kept in solitary confinement (often 23 hours a day) in small cells (typically 36-108 square feet), denied participation in programs, work, or other communal activities, have limited options for exercise (perhaps one hour a day, often in a cage-like enclosure), and are shackled and strip-searched when taken from their cells for severely limited visitation (American Civil Liberties Union, 2013). Quite obviously, such confinement, particularly when it endures year after year as time inches toward a scheduled execution, can and often does exact a serious toll on prisoners' physical and mental health.

Why are death rows like this? Officials may assume that individuals convicted of aggravated murder and sentenced to death are both extraordinarily dangerous and have nothing to lose by engaging in additional violence or attempting to escape from custody, and consequently must be confined under the most restrictive, highly secure conditions possible. Yet this assumption has not been borne out in practice in the few jurisdictions that have taken different approaches. In Missouri, for example, death-sentenced offenders, like others entering prison, are individually evaluated and then classified according to the security risk they present. The vast majority are assigned to the general prison population, where they intermingle with other inmates and are eligible for work, programs, exercise, and other privileges. Corrections officials have experienced no unusual behavioral or other difficulties under this policy (indeed, death-sentenced prisoners typically have fewer infractions and adapt better to prison life than other inmates), and in the process have realized considerable savings in terms of staffing and resources (Cunningham, Reidy & Sorensen, 2018). In North Carolina, death-sentenced prisoners are confined separately from other inmates, but they are allowed to interact among themselves and share in numerous communal activities (The Arthur Liman Public Interest Program, Yale Law School, 2016).

Prison administrators have the flexibility in almost all jurisdictions to implement policies like those in place in Missouri and North Carolina. Sadly, few have done so. As a result, thousands of death-sentenced offenders—most of whom spend years in solitary confinement and are likely to eventually be spared execution and re-sentenced to life imprisonment or even exonerated—have been denied vastly more humane living conditions. Regressive death row confinement endures despite evidence that alternative approaches are feasible from a security standpoint and yield considerable savings in staff and other resources.

References

American Civil Liberties Union (2013). *A Death Before Dying: Solitary Confinement on Death Row.* Available at https://www.aclu.org/sites/default/files/field_document/deathbeforedying-report.pdf

Baumgartner, FR, Davidson, M, Johnson, KR, Krishnamurthy, A & Wilson, CP (2018). *Deadly Justice: A Statistical Portrait of the Death Penalty.* New York: Oxford University Press.

Cunningham, MD, Reidy, TJ & Sorensen, JR (2018). The Failure of a Security Rationale for Death Row. In *Living on Death Row: The Psychology of Waiting to Die*, H Toch, J R Acker & VM. Bonventre, eds., pp. 129-159. Washington, DC: American Psychological Association.

Death Penalty Information Center (n.d.a). *Examples of Prisoners with Extraordinarily Long Stays on Death Row.* Available at https://deathpenaltyinfo.org/death-row/death-row-time-on-death-row/examples-of-prisoners-with-extraordinarily-long-stays-on-death-row

Death Penalty Information Center (n.d.b). *Innocence by the Numbers.* Available at https://deathpenaltyinfo.org/policy-issues/innocence/innocence-by-the-numbers

Gross, SR, O'Brien, B, Hu, C & Kennedy EH (2014). Rate of False Conviction of Criminal Defendants Who are Sentenced to Death. *Proceedings of the National Academy of Sciences, 111 (20):* 7230-7235. Available at https://www.pnas.org/content/111/20/7230

Liebman, JS, Fagan, J & West, V (2000). *A Broken System: Error Rates in Capital Cases, 1973-1995.* Available at https://scholarship.law.columbia.edu/cgi/viewcontent.cgi?article=2220&context=faculty_scholarship

Lozano, JA (2021). Longest Serving Death Row Inmate in US Resentenced to Life. Associated Press (June 9). Available at https://abcnews.go.com/US/wireStory/longest-serving-death-row-inmate-us-resentenced-life-78182097

Snell, TL (2021). *Capital Punishment, 2020—Statistical Tables* (US Dept. of Justice, Bureau of Justice Statistics). Available at https://bjs.ojp.gov/content/pub/pdf/cp20st.pdf

The Arthur Liman Public Interest Program, Yale Law School (2016). *Rethinking Death Row: Variations in the Housing of Individuals Sentenced to Death.* Available at https://law.yale.edu/sites/default/files/documents/pdf/Liman/deathrow_reportfinal.pdf

In Prison for Murder

Rick Sauve

Rick Sauve is a peer support worker for St. Leonard's Society. He provides one-to-one as well as group format services to prisoners in federal prisons in the Ontario region. He is also a prisoners' rights advocate, believing that providing hope can bring about positive change.

Dear Rick,

Wow, I found you. You probably don't remember me, but you were one of our mentors in juvenile detention. I hope you and your family are well. Sometimes you still cross my mind as the first man who ever gave me encouragement. Thank you, Rick. And thank you for all your efforts throughout the years helping young lost rug rats. I'm a better husband and father today partly because of you.

Take care, mentor.

Felix.

In 1978, I was arrested alongside seven other young men for committing murder. We were charged with a shooting that took place in a bar in a small town outside Toronto, where I was living at the time with my wife and daughter. The eight of us who were charged were members of the Satan's Choice Motorcycle Club. Six of us would eventually be convicted of murder, four in the second degree, and two of us, including myself, for murder in the first degree. Sadly, none of us was actually guilty. I refer you to Conspiracy of Brothers, an award-winning book by Mick Lowe, which chronicles the events of the night in question, the specifics of our court case, and the evidence that supports our innocence. We have all steadfastly maintained our innocence over the years.

I was handed a sentence of life in prison, with parole eligibility at twenty-five years. While I 'only' served seventeen years behind bars, much of which was in a maximum-security penitentiary, I never truly left the prison system. Perhaps the greatest illusion in our criminal justice system is that anyone truly stops serving time. Prison does not, and can never, escape me. I will always be known to the world as someone who was once convicted of murder.

Prison life is a world full of despair, violence and isolation. Worst of all, it can be a place devoid of hope. So many of the men I encountered during my seventeen years inside felt that they never had a stake in society. So many felt the sting of exclusion, be it from their experience in the education system, or having been shut out of normal community activities. Far too many had no grounding in family values; most came from broken homes and were primarily raised by a single parent, usually a mother, grandmother or aunt. Many had endured family abuse, and their upbringings were mired with violence or substance abuse. This is not to diminish one's personal responsibility in committing a crime, but it became clear to me that a tough upbringing was a consistent factor that had led so many of them down the road to prison.

When one is already cynical of society, feels disenfranchised, and lacks strong social support, it should be no surprise that adding an inherently isolating prison stay will only compound one's sense of hopelessness. And when prisoners lose hope, as so many do, they spend their time lashing out and rebelling, rather than focusing on any meaningful transformation. When such prisoners are then released, they continue to misbehave, and often end up back in prison. It's a self-perpetuating cycle.

Oddly enough, I consider myself one of the lucky ones. Despite my harsh sentence for a crime I did not commit, I had a supportive family that stood by me. It was my family's love and encouragement that willed me to go on. Their support gave me hope, and that hope is what staved off the despair and loneliness that consumed so many others. I sought to make the most of my time in prison. I completed my high school degree, earned a BA in psychology, and an honours degree in criminology. Becoming immersed in my studies enabled me to create a new kind of identity while living in prison. I kept as busy as I could, chairing several prisoner groups, inviting volunteers and community members to speak with us, and organizing charitable events. This all gave me purpose and allowed me to stay engaged with the outside world.

Much of my time was spent creating programs to deter at-risk youth from getting involved in violence and eventually landing themselves in prison. I co-developed Straight Talk, a program that trained men who were serving a life sentence to become mentors to youth who were starting to get in trouble in the criminal system (this should not be confused with The Scared Straight Program in the United States, which is a model I do not believe in at all). Mentors would go into schools and group homes to share their stories, and the youth participants were actually brought into the prisons to see our circumstances firsthand. Many of us mentors could see our past selves in those kids and, more importantly, the kids could see what a future in prison might look like if they failed to reflect and change their course in life.

I transitioned from prisoner to youth worker. It was in this capacity that I eventually met Felix, the young man who sent me the note at the beginning of this chapter. By being open and honest, I believed I could be a living example of how to change one's fate by staying focused on succeeding rather than accepting defeat. I was able to connect with the youth, not by preaching, but rather by listening, sharing and working collaboratively. It was not about meeting my expectations but helping them achieve their own. Felix was one of those kids who expressed to me that he just wanted to have a normal life, one in which he could fit in without always being pre-judged.

Upon being released from prison, I remember telling myself that I would never step back into a prison again. After all, why would I ever want to go back through the gates of hell I had yearned for so long to get out of? And, for a short while, I did detach, and immersed myself in a new career. But eventually, I started thinking about all those I had left behind inside. I started to have survivor's guilt. Like I said, prison never leaves you.

I have since devoted my life to working with prisoners still on the inside. To date, I have assisted in over five hundred parole hearings. I have taken hundreds of prisoners out on passes to the community. I have testified at sentencing hearings, and I have spoken a number of times at government and senate hearings regarding criminal justice and legislation. Much of my work focuses on helping newly released inmates integrate back into society. After so many years in prison, the rapidly evolving outside world can be an overwhelming place to navigate.

While I have found meaning in my career, it has come at a personal cost. I have lost a sense of normalcy living in the community, with prison still being such a part of my daily life. It often feels like I'm still serving time. Yes, I chose the work that I do, and nobody forces me to re-enter prisons and spend so much time with inmates. But even if I abandoned this work, prison would never leave me. Society still refers to me as a 'convicted person', and those who meet me will always know of my past. In spite of this, I do believe there is hope, that perhaps society can become more compassionate to former convicts, innocent or guilty, as they try to regain their footing in the world. Everyone has their own story, and so many work terribly hard to transform their lives. I hope the reader might consider giving those who have erred in the past a second chance at rehabilitation.

While my journey has been challenging, I live with the satisfaction that I have made a difference in so many people's lives, including the 'bookends', as I call them. The first bookend—Felix—is a young man in whose life I think I played an important part, perhaps leading him on a path away from the prison system. The second bookend—Billy—was a young man I met in prison while still serving time, who assisted me with some of my outreach work. He recently let me know how much he appreciated my standing by him and believing in him.

Dear Rick,

I just wanted to say hi and let you know I finally got it right out here. They gave me full parole without a hearing. I got a great job making great money, and have a great life with my daughter. I owe it all to you for believing in me and standing with me at my first parole hearing. You will always have a place in my heart, and I will always be forever grateful. I hope all is well in your world as you deserve it for giving so much to others.

Billy.

Indigenous Injustice

Morgan Fontaine

Theodore Niizhotay Fontaine was former Chief of Sagkeeng Anishinaabe First Nation, Knowledge Keeper, Elder, educator, leader and a survivor of 12 years of incarceration in Indian residential schools. His wife Morgan wrote this essay, based on Theodore's bestselling memoir, Broken Circle: The Dark Legacy of Indian Residential Schools, *and all that he shared with her privately and through more than 1,600 public presentations of his residential school experiences. Theodore reunited with his family in the spirit world in May 2021.*

Many non-Indigenous Canadians believe that Indian residential schools educated and saved Indian children—a long time ago. This erroneous thinking leads some to question why people who experienced Indian residential schools just don't 'get over it and move on with their lives'. After all, they suggest, these were schools, aimed at providing education to children.

It's as if they think Canada did not exist until Europeans arrived, claiming ownership of lands and resources and bringing their versions of 'civilization' to the lands they claimed to 'discover' and 'settle'.

It all comes down to who writes the history books, who tells the story, and who listens.

In reality, the lands of North America were populated by Indigenous peoples for thousands of years. But after Columbus famously got lost in 1492, Indigenous peoples were forced to defend themselves and their traditional territories. From the beginning, they were systematically removed, relocated and eradicated by force.

As the wealth of Canada's natural resources became known, decisions were made by Canada's government and ruling class to get Indigenous people out of the way of settlement, development and land ownership by non-Indigenous peoples. In a litany of genocidal actions, perhaps most tragic was the Indian residential schools policy.

The policy statement, read in Canada's Parliament, proposed that the way to get rid of Indians was to sever children from their families and communities, and force them to be ashamed of their beliefs of who they were, their connections with each other and with the land. The approved plan supposed that, after years of incarceration in industrial schools and, later, residential schools, the children would hate themselves and abandon their language, culture and communities.

The false message in schools taught children that their Indigenous cultures were savage and worthless, and that their families and heritage were far inferior to the rest of 'Canadians', as defined by White settlers. The goal was to make these children renounce their birthright and to prepare them to be fully utilized in the labor force as non-Indians.

The reality was that residential schools undertook the destruction of Indigenous children from the late 1800s until 1997, under the direction of the federal government and churches who executed the plan. Indigenous children were taken away from their families, their culture was eradicated, they were converted to Christianity, and they suffered unimaginable abuses and often died.

They say that history is written by the 'victors'. That is the history recorded in our dated history books. And so it is that the history of Canada, now revealed and recognized as colonial genocide, is a hard confrontation for a lot of people. This history dates back to the late 1400s with the arrival of Europeans in North America. When you examine the effects of colonization on the Indigenous peoples, there are clear, massively negative ramifications that occurred even before residential schools were imposed.

The economy of the Indigenous peoples was destroyed, lands seized, devastating diseases introduced, and animals and natural environments irrevocably damaged. The 1900s brought forth destruction of the people through Indian residential schools. This is 500 years of history culminating in the tragedy of what some still think of as 'education'—a cover to force Indigenous people to become something they can never be: White.

So where do we find truth and reconciliation? The truth is documented in the findings and calls to action of the Truth and Reconciliation Commission. But how far has Canada *actually* gone in acknowledging the truth? How far has it practically reconciled and made reparations for the damage that has been done? It depends on who you ask.

The testimonies of thousands of former students have been documented, recorded, presented and shared widely. Yet for those clinging to misconceptions about Canada's Indian residential schools, it seems they haven't heard about this true history. Some perhaps haven't listened, or have denied its existence, maintaining a long legacy of systemic racism and discriminatory beliefs and actions against Indigenous nations.

Perspectives are shaped and changed by the harrowing stories of residential school survivors and, more recently, by the discovery of apparent burials of children on residential school grounds. The information is readily available for those with intentions to learn the true, lived history of these schools, not the story told by the perpetrators of more than 500 years of colonization.

And yet, despite the documented reality of the residential school system and the traumas sustained by former students, all one needs to do is look around to challenge the false narrative that Indigenous peoples have simply 'lingered' on the past. You'll find Indigenous peoples widely represented in positions of leadership, government, academia, business, industry, nation-building, the corporate world, and more.

So, for those who claim that Indigenous people just 'can't get over Indian residential schools', just think, or read, or listen, before you say: "Why can't they just get over it!"

The true history is there for the asking.

And consider this—would you "just get over it" if it were your young children or grandchildren forcibly seized to be institutionalized by a foreign power aiming to make them over into something they're not?

References

Fontaine, Theodore Niizhotay, *Broken Circle, The Dark Legacy of Indian Residential Schools* (2010, 2022), Heritage House Publishing Company Ltd.

Assiniboia Residential School Legacy Group, *Did You See Us? Reunion, Remembrance, and Reclamation at an Urban Indian Residential School (2021)*, University of Manitoba Press.

Fontaine, Theodore, *Foreword, Stolen Lives, The Indigenous Peoples of Canada and the Indian Residential Schools* (2015), Facing History and Ourselves.

Fontaine, Theodore, *Foreword, Colonial Genocide in Indigenous North America* (2014), Duke University Press.

Mind and Body

Yoga: Not Just Exercise
Hypnosis
The Boxer
Japanese Culture: The Space Between the Stems

Yoga: Not Just Exercise

Karina Guthrie

Karina Guthrie is a yoga teacher trainer and women's wellbeing coach with more than a decade of experience under her belt. Her passion is to empower others to transform their lives from the inside out using the ancient wisdom and practices of the yoga tradition.

*"I am not the mind,
I am the awareness that observes my mind thinking"*

I remember when I first began to practice yoga. It was purely a physical pursuit. I wanted to become stronger and more flexible, so I found myself chasing 'advanced' poses that I couldn't do yet but wanted to do.

I remember, around that time, reaching a roadblock in the form of a pose. This pose became my arch nemesis. Teacher after teacher said to me, "There is no reason you can't get into this pose." Each time I heard that, I thought, "There obviously *is* a reason, otherwise I'd be in it."

One day, a few seconds before attempting the pose for the second time that class, I found myself complaining in my head, "My legs are too heavy, my muscles are too weak." Then another thought entered my mind: "What would the pose feel like if I actually managed to do it?"

Where would my weight be placed? Would my legs still feel heavy?

What would my mind be doing?

I imagined it.

The teacher cued the pose again and suddenly… I was in it. Not the struggling half-in-half-out version from a few minutes before; a full this-couldn't-have-been-any-easier version that I'd never experienced before.

The only thing that changed was how I thought about the pose. Such is the power of the mind.

This was my first yoga breakthrough, though it certainly wasn't the last. The body (through the medium of yoga's physical practices) has been the vehicle for many of those breakthroughs. Ultimately, though, as my practice has matured, the physical aspects have become less important.

Looking back, the reason that day was significant was that it showed me the depths of my unrealized potential. Yoga has a lot to say about this. Its teaching is that we operate from only the smallest portion of our potential. The greater portion of our potential exists in unmanifest form. Our job, then, is to clear out the barriers to its realization.

Those barriers take the form of cultural conditioning, self-limiting beliefs, the 'shoulda, coulda, woulda' stories we tell ourselves in our head. All these stories have been *learned* from family, from friends, from society. It stands to reason, then, that if learned, they can be *unlearned* too.

The stories we tell ourselves about ourselves tend to make our experience smaller. The practices we undertake in yoga (whether they're physical, psychological or spiritual) are there, not in service of a tighter butt or longer hamstrings, but to the refinement of our capacity for clear seeing. They help us see truth from fiction, real from unreal.

As our awareness expands, our life expands too.

Will our butt become tighter or our hamstrings longer in the process? Probably, but why stop there? Physical practices are a drop in the ocean of yoga, and if you've ever derived value from the drop, imagine what you might find in the ocean.

What I learned that day on the mat is that my mind is both my greatest obstacle and most powerful ally. If I think the mind is all I am, I will be a slave to the thoughts it produces. If, on the other hand, I come to understand that 'mind' is something I *have*, not something I *am*, the entire playing field shifts.

Many questions arise from a shift like this.

For example, when I realise that I am not my mind, but the awareness observing the mind thinking, I am catapulted into deep contemplation about who I am, my place in the world and the meaning of my own existence.

Welcome.

Now you're doing yoga.

Hypnosis

Luke Chao

Luke Chao founded The Morpheus Clinic for Hypnosis in 2006, after graduating from the University of Toronto with a degree in English literature. He can be found explaining hypnosis on YouTube and sharing his life philosophy on TikTok, both @morpheushypnosis.

Every hypnotist knows that the first thing you must do with a new client is dispel any misconceptions. Since we need the client's cooperation, they can't start with the wrong idea about how hypnosis will work, or their progress could be hampered by fear, mistrust or passivity.

Most of the common misconceptions about hypnosis fall into two opposing categories: either that hypnosis is less powerful than it actually is, or that hypnosis is more powerful than it actually is. Those who believe it's less powerful than it is think of hypnosis as a placebo at best, like much of alternative medicine. Those who believe it's more powerful think hypnosis can force people to do things against their will, that it gives people supernatural powers, or that it's otherwise 'magic'. Sometimes, you'll find both beliefs in the same person ("Don't try that hypnosis stuff on me: it's not going to work.").

In the modern world, the value of subjective experience is often overlooked in favour of what can be measured objectively. Even though we each live in our own subjective experiences, our inner realms are largely outside the purview of science and medicine. That's how "it's a placebo" became synonymous with "it doesn't work" in many people's minds, even though the placebo effect must be controlled for in clinical trials precisely because it causes participants to experience actual relief! Hypnosis works through the power of suggestion too, but, unlike placebos, there is no element of deceit—we might be the only profession that explicitly tells clients we are using the power of suggestion—and our verbal suggestions can give more specific guidance than a sugar pill or saline injection. If we acknowledge that our subjective experiences matter, we can no longer dismiss hypnosis or the power of suggestion simply because it works through an unseen psychological mechanism.

The state we call hypnosis allows the client to suspend their usual mode of thinking and accept new ideas more readily. It feels like an intensified version of the state you're in when you're listening wholeheartedly to your favourite instructor or storyteller. The ideas being suggested should (at least in my view) be truthful and reassuring, or truthful and empowering, never fantasy or wishful thinking. Quality ideas are easy to accept regardless of how hypnotized the client is, while unhelpful ideas aren't worth accepting at any depth. The good news is that hypnosis doesn't make people *completely* suggestible even when it makes them *more* suggestible. If the hypnotist makes a suggestion that you find objectionable, you won't accept it, and you will probably start to question everything else they have to say, too.

As it turns out, many 'medical' problems (and many more non-medical problems) benefit from a change in attitude and sometimes even resolve completely when you think about them differently. For example, when a smoker fully embraces the thoughts and views of a non-smoker, smoking no longer feels right, the way that stepping outside for a breath of fresh air does. When an insomniac is able to adopt the mindset of somebody who enjoys bedtime and looks forward to their sleep, they will feel less anxiety and fall asleep more easily. When somebody who has irritable bowel syndrome starts to trust their body and communicate with their gut the same way they would speak to a friend, they will feel more comfortable with their body and experience a higher quality of life. Hypnosis makes it easier to accept these new ways of thinking, but it's the new ways of thinking that cause long-term change.

In short, hypnosis isn't fake, nor is it magic. If you understand hypnotism as the skillful use of verbal suggestions to help people turn inwardly and accept new ideas, you will understand its power without overestimating its capabilities.

The Boxer

Mark Simmons

Mark Simmons is an eight-year National Boxing Team member, Commonwealth Games gold medalist, Pan Am Games silver medalist, and quarter-finalist at the 2000 Olympic Games. Mark completed his Bachelor of Science in Kinesiology and Health Science at York University in 2000.

Let me put something out there that is quite obvious: the sport of boxing can be very dangerous. Boxers have died in the ring, and many end up with injuries that impact them for the rest of their lives. Every few years, medical doctors call for a ban on the sport when a boxer dies from punishment sustained in the ring. However, simply looking negatively at this sport through tinted glasses is not nearly enough to understand why we so badly need to continue to embrace it and realize that boxing actually saves more lives than it takes.

While history is not enough to justify a sport, it does provide some context to understanding boxing in the present day. Fighting matches go back to ancient Roman times, and in many ways combat seems to be inherent to human nature. Martial arts such as boxing have created better skill sets for one to get the upper hand and accomplish victory. It wasn't until 1865 when boxing first became recognized as an official sport, when John Graham Chambers drafted the Marquess of Queensberry Rules. These rules ultimately defined and set the parameters for the sport, dictating the length of rounds, ring size, the wearing of gloves, and so forth.

To the untrained eye, a boxing match is just two foes swinging for the fences, trying to knock one another out with every punch they throw. Boxing purists, in contrast, have often called the sport 'The Sweet Science', a term used to describe how boxers need to be technical and have a game plan to win a match. Many actually compare the sport to a chess match, where one fighter meticulously tries to break down his adversary to ultimately expose flaws in his opponent's tactics.

In addition to the long history and skillset needed to succeed in the sport, the social value of boxing trumps any negative judgment one can put on it. My personal journey may be different to most that enter the sport, as I grew up in a stable household in a good neighbourhood. The problem my parents had was that I had too much energy and nothing I did seemed to burn it off. Although I was an active kid in many sports, my personality required something more. To burn off energy, my parents would send me out the door to run around the block; when they realized I still wasn't tired, they'd encourage me to do it again! Today, medical doctors might have prescribed a hyperactive kid like myself with some type of medication, but my parents' solution was physical activity and, eventually, my dad took me down to a boxing gym where I found a home.

Boxing gyms have always been a home for lost youth to find a sense of purpose in life. We all know the story of 12-year-old Mike Tyson. After committing armed robbery, he was sent to juvenile detention, where he was mentored by Cus D'Amato, who ran a boxing gym located on top of a police station. The list of boxers that have come from similar situations and found their way to a boxing gym is endless.

Now switch me with a child growing up in a neighbourhood ravaged by poverty, drugs and gang violence, and you have the recipe for someone who will end up going down the wrong path in life. Kids raised under such circumstances often don't fare well at school and emulate what they see around them. We cannot deny that the future of a child growing up in such an environment doesn't bode well for them, and unless that negative energy is put towards something more positive, the cycle will repeat.

In order to have success in boxing, one must physically train extremely hard, learn discipline, and be consistent in their training every day. In effect, there isn't as much time to be sidetracked by trouble, especially when you know that you need to be up at 6am to do your roadwork. More importantly, you are now building a sense of purpose, and a misguided soul now knows that the most important task in his life is to train towards the next competition. Many young people have never experienced personal success, and failing at school can be psychologically demoralizing, but stepping inside a boxing ring can help build character and confidence in a child who struggles to focus on other aspects of life.

Whether one has developed a heightened amount of anger, fear or aggression during their young life, an environment like a boxing gym is the perfect place to learn how to work through those emotions. Connecting with a teenager can be tough at the best of times but imagine one who has grown up in poverty and crime. The relationship between coach and fighter cannot be underestimated, as the coach is often the most influential person in that youth's life. Often that child just needs to know that somebody else cares about them, that they are important, and that somebody wants to make a difference in their life.

Yes, you can get hurt in boxing, but the same goes for many other sports, such as football and hockey. Boxing plays a role for those personalities that perhaps don't take to team sports and require a safe place to more responsibly defuse some of that anger and aggression. Life is full of failures and successes, but like in a boxing ring, you can't keep walking into punches. You need to take your time and assess the task that is directly in front of you. For many youths, boxing helps them understand how to focus on one punch at a time by putting them in a stable environment, instead of worrying about the outside world, where life may be a lot more dangerous than simply having to dodge your opponents' fists.

Japanese Culture: The Space Between the Stems

Erin Niimi Longhurst

Erin Niimi Longhurst is a British/Japanese author, based in London. Her written work to date has been largely inspired by her dual heritage; her books, Japonisme *(2018) and* Omoiyari *(2020) are published by HarperCollins.*

It's a complicated business, making things look simple.

This weekend, I went to watch a practitioner of *Ikebana* at work.

Ikebana is the centuries-old practice of Japanese floral design, an art form that constantly, in my opinion, defies preconceptions. A leisurely pursuit, you might think, for those with too much time. A pastime for those who are delicate.

Like Ikebana, many Japanese rituals can be easily misunderstood.

Behind the seeming simplicity of these traditions, it can be easy to miss the detailed nuance. In reality, it is actually the complexity and detail of these rituals that underly the beautiful simplicity that results. *Sado*, a traditional tea ceremony, is not just about drinking tea. *Kintsugi*—the restoration of broken pottery—is not just about repairing ceramics. And *Shinrin-Yoku*—forest therapy—is not just taking a walk in the forest.

There are several schools of Ikebana, the literal translation of which is 'giving life to flowers'. It's not just about enhancing and celebrating the beauty of nature but exceeding it. By pruning, cutting and arranging, you're not demonstrating how things are, but how things *should* be—according to your point of view. By including stems and branches that might be decaying, you remind the viewer of the transient nature of things. The materials you use in Ikebana often include dying materials, but fresh buds, too—things might wither and fade, but they have ephemeral beauty. When you create an arrangement, you create a statement and, more often than not, it reminds the viewer: 'memento mori'.

While one might consider floral arrangements to be a dainty art form, one suitable for those with delicate wrists and hushed voices, it is really anything but.

There are different forms arrangements can take, you see. It's a delicate art, yet arrangements created in the more ostentatious *Rikka* style require the practitioner to employ a range of power tools and hacksaws to get the desired result.

As I watched the diminutive instructor run through several demonstrations over the weekend, I was astounded by her strength as she lifted heavy branches, which seemed to be half her weight, and shaped their form with apparent fluidity and ease. It seemed second nature to her.

There was nothing weak or delicate about her command of the practice. In that hour, I saw more strength and resilience than in anyone I've seen obsessively pumping iron at the gym.

It's said that army generals would often practice Ikebana as a way to strategize before a battle. By focusing on the stems and natural material in front of them, it gave the practitioner the mental clarity to see where the path was leading. In Ikebana, the more simple arrangements, which use fewer stems, are often the most challenging.

On the surface, it looks simple. But acquiring the ability to evoke the sense you want through stems and bulbs that have grown from seed is anything but. It requires hours, days, years of insight and practice.

It's a humbling process. Those who are devoted to the art form find that they continue to learn, decades into their practice. This is something I think we can all benefit from: the ability to keep an open mind, savour that inquisitiveness, and constantly ask questions of yourself and others. This understanding is core to a true appreciation of what is offered by the array of Japanese crafts and traditions that are practiced with such dedicated concentration.

Simple doesn't mean easy, and it doesn't mean quick. There are always hidden depths to explore—especially in the space between the stems.

Unwell

Depression
My OCD
The Opioid Crisis
Dopamine Nation
HIV: My Fabulous Disease
COVID Rehab

Depression

Joshua Rivedal

Joshua Rivedal—speaker, actor, playwright, and stand-up comic—is the creator and founder of Changing Minds: A Mental Health Based Curriculum and The i'Mpossible Project. He has spoken about suicide prevention and mental health across the US, Canada, the UK, and Australia. www.iampossibleproject.com

As a mental health educator and someone who lives with two mental illnesses—clinical depression and generalized anxiety disorder—I wish more people had a clearer understanding of what mental illness is and isn't. Most of the time, my mental illnesses don't really affect me on a major level. They're a little like background noise in my daily life; I can treat them as such, still paying them some attention, because I've worked hard over the past ten years to live and grow with them. To give you a clearer idea of what depression *can* look like, I want to introduce you to mine, sharing how I began to really work with my depression during a painful period in 2018.

★ ★ ★

Hey, dummy. You can't keep trying to run away from me. I'm always gonna be with you. She's divorcing you. She doesn't love you. You don't love you. You're nothing. You're worse than nothing. You're my bitch.

"Easy. I… I think she still loves me… and so do other people. I'm just tired—and sad. And I am not your bitch."

Yeah? Why are you here again? Sad. Miserable. Lonely. Take a drink. Take twenty. You'll feel better.

"No. Shut the hell up. Why are you so pissed off, anyway?"

Haha. It's none of your damn business.

"I'm calling… a friend. I don't need this right now."

★ ★ ★

That's my depression talking. I've been living with this character my entire life—though we only met formally after I turned twenty-seven. His name is Dewayne. He can be cool sometimes, but other times he can be an arrogant d-bag.

And all this extra negativity coming from him? As of the past six months or so, it's kinda my fault. The pain of this divorce is taking a toll. I also haven't been taking Dewayne on regular walks or working out with him like I should. We do like the same music, but lately, I haven't been listening to the kind he likes. And he's mad that I haven't been feeding him healthy food, either. Right now, I'm holding a bottle of vodka in one hand and a glass of ice in the other, but I haven't poured it yet.

Sometimes, I try to use vodka to shut Dewayne up—it never works for long. Lately, it's just made him louder and angrier. So, I've cut back the booze pretty drastically. Except I found a half-empty bottle at the bottom of my pantry the other day. And now Dewayne is practically screaming at me that we finish it together. So tempting.

★ ★ ★

Just pour the damn drink and be done with it already. When you drink, your problems go away.

"And they come right back in the morning—we've been through this a million times."

Yeah, papi—but this time it'll be different. I promise. See? Good boy. Pour it. Put it to your lips. Good boy..."

"No," I say, slamming my drink on the kitchen counter and then pouring it down the drain. "I won't this time. I'm going outside."

That's my boy. A cigarette. Finally, something we can both enjoy.

★ ★ ★

Dewayne is right. We both find temporary pleasure in nicotine. I've quit that too but found an old pack today in the nightstand on the side where *she* used to sleep.

I haven't been taking care of him or myself lately. So, I take one of her old cigarettes out onto the balcony. I inhale the first drag of tar, nicotine and pure, momentary bliss. Dewayne is loving life right now, too. But my lungs and heart, however, are both incredibly angry with me. They're threatening to go on strike if I don't quit smoking for good. Unlike Dewayne, both my lungs and heart have asked that their names be withheld for privacy purposes.

★ ★ ★

Why are we back inside? I'm already bored. I can just keep making fun of you... or... you can start hitting yourself. Remember when you used to do that?

"It's not going to help get us what we want or what we need."

★ ★ ★

It's tough to admit this, but from ages six to thirteen, Dewayne used to tell me it was okay to slap myself in the head repeatedly when things got too intense at home or when I couldn't solve a homework problem. Eventually, I figured out how to tell Dewayne that physically hurting myself wasn't good, and I stopped. But lately, he's been tempting me to start again.

★ ★ ★

I see you looking at that bottle of medication. That would be easy. Do it like your dad did.

"No. We're not going back to that place. It's been nine years, and it'll be another six hundred."

Such a drama queen.

★ ★ ★

Dewayne isn't all bad. I've had to fight so hard against him my whole life that he's helped serve as sort of a rocket away from the feeling that I'm worthless. He can be encouraging at times. He even lets me talk about him in public, because he knows he hurts me and feels bad about it sometimes.

★ ★ ★

So, you're sad. So, you're not getting what you want. Why even try?

"You're not my enemy. You're my friend. We've been through this before and we've made it out."

Alright... What do we do? What did we do last time?

"Well, we've got to get back into therapy. Maybe you and I do couples counseling," I say, going down the list of what I call my *resiliency toolbox*. "Get back into taekwondo. Fewer fried foods. Be vulnerable with the people we love. Manage expectations. Work on self-esteem. And we've got to be in constant communication. If you're not feeling good, I'm not feeling good. You've got to speak up sooner, and so do I. Deal?"

Fine. But less talk-y and more run-y. Get your running shoes, Mr I'm-Gonna-Take-Action. Hurry your ass up.

"Chill. I'm putting on my running gear as fast as I can. What should we listen to while jogging? Coldplay?"

You know me too well. 'Viva la Vida' is my jam, yo.

"Let's roll," I say, as we take off into the streets of southern Los Angeles, the moon and the streetlights as our only guides.

My OCD

Dr Zale Mednick

Zale Mednick is the creator and host of the podcast Preconceived, *the inspiration for this book. He is a practicing ophthalmologist in Toronto, Canada.*

"That thought is absolutely totally done forever. I'm never ever going to think about that thought ever again, never ever again. I can relax and enjoy myself for the rest of the day, for the rest of the night, for the rest of the night, for the rest of the day, and forever. That thought is absolutely totally done forever. Done."

This is a phrase I have repeated to myself literally thousands of times in my life. If I have the luxury of privacy, I might repeat the phrase out loud to quell my anxiety. If in public, though, as I often am when the anxiety strikes, I simply repeat the phrase in my mind as many times as I need to until the anxiety abates. Usually nobody notices. If I'm in a particularly heightened state, I might go to the washroom or the corner of the room and mumble the phrase quietly so nobody can hear me. But for the most part, I'm quite 'talented' at hiding my compulsions. Most people who know me, even some of my closest friends, have no idea that I live with Obsessive Compulsive Disorder (OCD). And that is no fault of theirs. It is a testament to the internal nature of OCD, and how the disease does not always manifest in the outwardly obvious ways one might expect. It's easy to assume that we know what is going on in others' lives. Even if we cannot read their exact thoughts, we tend to think that if something were truly wrong, we would probably know about it or have some inclination. Perhaps nowhere is this misconception greatest as when it relates to mental illness. While OCD and most psychiatric illnesses do manifest externally, the symptoms can often be well-hidden from even one's closest social circle.

Obsessive Compulsive Disorder is, unsurprisingly, characterized by obsessions and compulsions (hence the exceedingly clever name). When people think of OCD, they probably conjure up an image of someone vigorously scrubbing their hands with an excessive amount of soap. And while handwashing by no means encompasses all facets of OCD, it serves as a useful example to explain the disease. One becomes 'obsessed' with the idea that their hands are dirty. This obsession leads to anxiety, a fear that they themselves are unclean or, worse, that they might contaminate someone else. To subdue the anxiety, they engage in the 'compulsion' of washing their hands to cleanse themselves of the supposed contamination. Washing their hands might indeed help repress the anxiety, but such relief is typically only temporary. In fact, engaging in the compulsion only serves to strengthen the obsession in the long term. The more one indulges in the compulsion of handwashing, the greater the credence given to the obsession of contamination. And so, despite the momentary relief, the obsession returns with a greater vengeance, and more handwashing is required. Untreated, this cycle will continue indefinitely, with stronger conviction of one's contamination leading to more frequent and vigorous handwashing.

I have done my fair share of handwashing in my day—been there, done that—but, like many people with OCD, the disease has manifested for me in a variety of other ways. My OCD has primarily expressed itself in the form of guilt. When my OCD was at its heights, I would feel guilty about pretty much everything: looking at someone a moment too long, giving off an almost certainly imperceptible sign of impatience, or not having thanked someone sufficiently for a nice deed. Usually, somewhere deep down, I was able to realize that I hadn't done anything wrong. That's what I still find so fascinating about OCD. The patient often retains insight into the reality of the situation. The handwasher usually knows deep down that they are acting irrationally—that their hands are indeed clean. Part of me usually acknowledges that I have nothing to feel guilty about, that the obsession itself is irrational. Nonetheless, the anxiety that I have done something wrong feels so real that I have no choice but to indulge it. In such situations, I might engage in such compulsions like apologizing to the person in question or, more often, silently repeating certain phrases in my mind in order to rationalize that I haven't done anything wrong. Let me share with you an example.

I was nineteen years old, standing in line for a coffee during a short break from one of my lectures in my second year at university. There were two cashiers: one was White, and one was Black. When my turn arrived, the White cashier opened up and I proceeded to walk towards her. But when the Black cashier opened up a mere second or two later, I knew I was in trouble. Immediately, the thoughts stormed into my mind. "Why did you choose the White cashier? It must be because you're racist. That's right, you're a racist and a bad person." The guilt quickly escalated. My anxiety was palpable. My chest was tight, my breathing was labored and, worse than anything, I developed an insufferable headache from spinning thoughts of confusion and self-chastising. My obsession was that I was a racist. But any good obsession needs an equally convincing compulsion to stave it off, right? I went with my go-to compulsion—internal rationalization.

"Zale, you aren't racist. The White cashier opened up a couple seconds before the Black cashier, and that's why you went to her. Even if they had both become free at the exact same moment, you had to choose someone, and it doesn't make you racist simply because you had to 'choose' one over the other. You've done nothing to suggest that you're racist, and this one example should have no bearing on your life or the lives of the cashiers. This is a story you've completely created in your head."

I don't remember the exact monologue, but I'm sure this went on for several minutes in my head. Eventually, I must have reached a transient state of relief, at which point I proceeded to my all-encompassing well-rehearsed concluding phrase that I shared earlier.

"That thought is absolutely totally done forever. I'm never ever going to think about that thought ever again, never ever again. I can relax and enjoy myself for the rest of the day, for the rest of the night, for the rest of the night, for the rest of the day, and forever. That thought is absolutely totally done forever. Done."

I probably flicked my hand at the end of this phrase, to reflect the finality with which the thought was gone. But, unsurprisingly, my compulsion was ineffective. The obsession would recur shortly thereafter, the anxiety would return, and I would replay the sequence of events and the rationalization of my innocence tens of times over the course of the next day. I would find a way to function in between these compulsory internal dialogues, but there would be a baseline level of angst that continued to consume me. Eventually, my anxiety would subside, but only after hours of exhaustible mental fatigue.

Keep in mind that this 'cashier incident' took place in a very busy coffee shop. The internal rationalizations were all done in public. Perhaps my monologue was put on pause for a brief moment if I saw a friend and was forced to make pleasantries, but they would have had no idea that anything was wrong. Aside from maybe seeming consumed in my thoughts, nobody would have had a clue. This was all in my head.

OCD is in many ways a silent disorder. Yes—repeated handwashing, spending hours cleaning, and triple checking plans with someone might be tougher to conceal. But there is a whole dimension of OCD that occurs solely in the mind. Like many psychiatric disorders, the suffering that those experience with OCD is often not visible—not to the public, nor to close friends and family. The truth is that nobody ever really knows what is going on in someone's mind. In some ways, that's a blessing. In other ways, it makes living with OCD more challenging. Ultimately, all we can do is try and show as much empathy and compassion as possible to those we love, for we never truly know how much they might need it.

The Opioid Crisis

Dr Sarah Elliott

Sarah Elliott is a family doctor working in Calgary, Alberta. She has a background in health promotion and enhanced skill training in addiction medicine. She serves primarily an urban, low-income, homeless/precariously housed population and aims to advocate for healthy public policy that improves health equity.

One of the public health crises of this century continues, and I am not referring to the COVID-19 pandemic. The attention, resources and political will to address our other public health emergency, the opioid crisis, pale in comparison to that of the global pandemic, despite some jurisdictions and age groups suffering substantially more morbidity and mortality from opioid poisoning.

Throughout North America, mortality from opioid poisoning is increasing at an alarming rate. Between April 2020 and March 2021, Canada saw a 95% increase in opioid poisoning deaths when compared to the year prior, with 20 Canadians dying each day of opioid poisoning.[5] Once a crisis of overprescribed and diverted prescription opioids, most of the morbidity and mortality now stems from an unregulated illicit drug supply of toxic fentanyl and even more potent

---

[5] Government of Canada. (2022). Opioid- and Stimulant-related Harms in Canada. Retrieved from https://health-infobase.canada.ca/substance-related-harms/opioids-stimulants/

fentanyl analogues, including carfentanil. For reference, fentanyl is approximately one hundred times stronger than morphine. This toxic opioid supply is increasingly contaminated with sedatives, including benzodiazepines, a dangerous mix which can lead to respiratory depression and overdose death.

As the opioid crisis continues unabated, killing siblings, children, friends and parents, is it reasonable to ask, "Does the public really care?" If you ask any politician, or any citizen for that matter, the answer will likely be: "Of course I care." But, given the severity of the current opioid crisis, has feigning concern just become the politically correct thing to do? Or is there something unique to the opioid crisis that makes people care less or become less engaged in finding/fighting for a solution?

One of the reasons this public health emergency is so challenging to address is the stigmatization associated with addiction and mental health. Part of this stigma, I argue, stems from how we address addiction throughout much of the world. We criminalize it.

To understand addiction, we need to consider the root causes. Approximately 50% of vulnerability to addiction can be attributed to genetic factors, not dissimilar to other chronic health conditions. The other determinants of addiction include but are not limited to trauma—particularly adversity in early childhood including experiencing violence, abuse and/or neglect before age 18—and concurrent mental illness.

We also know that someone experiencing addiction has progressive structural and functional disruptions in brain regions responsible for motivation, reward and inhibitory control, which make 'just quitting' without significant support nearly impossible to do. Many of the people I see want nothing more than to get well but suggesting that the patient has the free will to stop using is a failure to understand addiction's neurobiological impacts. Those with physiologic dependence to substances such as opioids suffer severe withdrawal symptoms during detox, limiting its success. And detoxification, when used alone, is associated with an increase in mortality due to a rapid change in opioid tolerance and subsequent high risk of relapse and opioid overdose.

Addiction is clearly a health issue. It is rooted in genetics, epigenetics, and the social determinants of health. It alters brain chemistry and signalling. Yet society at large views substance users as being in a moral crisis, not a health crisis. We talk about free will and responsibility, not urgent medical/psychiatric needs and safety. When someone presents with a heart attack, we don't suggest they are at fault. We don't blame them for their faulty genetics, cholesterol intake, physical inactivity and/or stress levels. We treat them with evidence and empathy—good medicine. Yet when we approach people struggling with addiction, we treat them as if they have done something wrong—as if their gene pool, their trauma in early childhood, their suffering is their fault.

This is in part because our approach to substance use has been to treat it as a criminal justice issue. Instead of *treating* our substance-addicted community members, they are often incarcerated—where their traumas are intensified, and they are further isolated and marginalized from family, friends and community. They are often denied access to the standard of care for their substance use disorder and concurrent mental illness.

Once their sentence is complete, they now have a criminal record, limiting their ability to access basic needs such as housing and employment, and often impacting their ability to see their children, travel and, in some areas, even vote. Impaired by this criminal record, they have yet another barrier to achieving wellness.

Worse, the traumatization and functional impairment associated with incarceration is not experienced equitably throughout our society. Systemic racism within our criminal justice system results in over-representation of racialized North Americans in the prison system.

At a systems level, the pressures of criminalization result in more potent drugs in smaller volumes in order to evade detection. This intensifies the toxicity of the supply and increases the profit and power of organized crime, thereby further harming community stability.

Taken all together, one can see how it is not surprising that the opioid situation is worsening. Addiction is still stigmatized, and the approach of criminalization is not only misguided but counterproductive in helping these patients get better.

Part of the answer to our current opioid crisis lies in decriminalizing simple possession of drugs for personal use. Decriminalization should not be misinterpreted as suggesting that drug use is not risky. Decriminalization aims to do exactly the opposite; it recognizes the dangerousness of these substances and reduces barriers for people to find the help they need.

Stigma kills. Criminalization kills. It's time to treat the opioid crisis as we treat other health emergencies: with evidence and with empathy… In other words, with good medicine. I do believe that many people truly do care about the opioid crisis. But I also believe that the ever-present stigma regarding addiction and a subconscious bias against those who suffer from substance use disorders has ultimately left this crisis relatively neglected for far too long.

Dopamine Nation

Anna Lembke, MD

Dr Anna Lembke is a professor of psychiatry and addiction medicine at Stanford University School of Medicine, and author, most recently, of Dopamine Nation: Finding Balance in the Age of Indulgence *(Dutton PRH, 2021).*

Over the past 50 years, rates of depression, anxiety and suicide have gone up all over the world, especially in rich nations.

According to the World Happiness Report, which ranks 156 countries by how happy their citizens perceive themselves to be, people living in the United States reported being less happy in 2018 than they were in 2008. Other countries with similar measures of wealth, social support and life expectancy saw similar decreases in self-reported happiness scores, including Belgium, Canada, Denmark, France, Japan, New Zealand and Italy.

Researchers interviewed nearly 150,000 people in twenty-six countries to determine the prevalence of generalized anxiety disorder, defined as excessive and uncontrollable worry that adversely affected their life. They found that richer countries had higher rates of anxiety than poor ones.

The authors wrote, "The number of new cases of depression worldwide increased 50 percent between 1990 and 2017. The highest increases in new cases were seen in regions with the highest sociodemographic index (income), especially North America."

This is a paradox, because you would think that having more of everything we need and want would make us happier. In fact, it seems to have done the opposite. How can we understand this?

The neuroscience of pleasure and pain offers one explanation.

One of the most important discoveries in the field of neuroscience in the past 100 years is that pleasure and pain are co-located. By that, I mean the same parts of the brain that process pleasure also process pain. And pleasure and pain work like a balance. When we feel pleasure, the balance tips one way; when we feel pain, it tips the other. One of the overarching rules governing this balance is that it wants to stay level. After any deviation from neutrality, our brains will work very hard to restore a level balance, or what neuroscientists call 'homeostasis'.

For example, I like to watch YouTube videos of *American Idol*. When I watch, my brain releases a little bit of the neurotransmitter dopamine in my brain's reward pathway and my balance tips slightly to the side of pleasure. But no sooner has that happened than my brain adapts to the increased dopamine by down-regulating my own dopamine receptors and dopamine transmission. I like to imagine this as little gremlins hopping on the pain side of my balance to bring it level again. (Not very scientific, I know.)

But here's the thing about those gremlins: they like it on the balance. So, they don't hop off once it's level. They stay on until it has tipped an equal and opposite amount to the side of pain. This is the after-effect, the hangover, the comedown, or, in my case, that moment of wanting to watch just one more video. If I wait long enough, the gremlins hop off the balance, neutrality is restored, and that feeling passes.

But what if I don't wait? What if, instead, I watch another video, and another, and another? Pretty soon I'm no longer watching *American*

Idol YouTube videos, I'm watching YouTube videos of people watching YouTube videos alternating with memes of Dr Pimple Popper. If I keep doing this for hours a day, days to weeks, weeks to months, I end up with enough gremlins on the pain side of my balance to fill a whole room. They're camped out for the long haul, tents and barbecues in tow. Once that happens, I've changed my hedonic (joy) set-point. I'm in a dopamine-deficit state. I need to keep watching YouTube videos not to feel pleasure, but just to feel normal. As soon as I stop watching, I experience the universal symptoms of withdrawal from any addictive substance: anxiety, irritability, insomnia, dysphoria, and mental preoccupation with using, otherwise known as craving. This is the hallmark of the addicted brain.

This fine-tuned balance of ours has evolved over millions of years to help us approach pleasure and avoid pain. It's what has kept us alive in a world of scarcity and ever-present danger. But here's the problem. We no longer live in that world. We now live in a world of overwhelming abundance. The access, quantity, variety and potency of highly reinforcing drugs and behaviors has never been greater—including drugs that didn't exist before: texting/tweeting, gaming/gambling, sugar/shopping, vaping/voyeuring… The list is endless. Online products, with their flashing lights, celebratory sounds, laudatory 'Likes', bottomless bowls, and the promise of ever-greater rewards just a finger-click away, are engineered to be addictive. The smartphone is the equivalent of the hypodermic needle, delivering digital dopamine for a wired generation. If you haven't met your drug yet, it's coming soon to a website near you.

So, what to do about it?

First, avoid intoxicants, or, if you do use them, use in small amounts and leave enough time in between for the balance to reset itself.

Second, recognize that in the modern world almost everything has been 'drugified', from food to human connection, so be a wary consumer.

Third, invite discomfort and pain into your life as a way to reset your balance to the side of pleasure. This is known as the science of hormesis. Exposure to mild to moderate noxious stimuli, like exercise, ice-cold temperatures and hunger, tells the body to protect itself by increasing production of our own feel-good hormones and neurotransmitters, like dopamine, serotonin and norepinephrine. It's a way of feeling good by doing the hard work up front and basking in the aftermath, an ultimately healthier way to get our dopamine.

Bottom line. Pleasure leads to pain. Pain leads to pleasure. In a world of overwhelming access to an infinite supply of pleasure stimuli, it's time to abstain and reacquaint ourselves with pain.

HIV: My Fabulous Disease

Mark S King

Mark S King won the GLAAD Media Award for his ongoing blog, My Fabulous Disease, which chronicles his life as a long-term HIV survivor. His book A Place Like This *is a memoir about coming of age in Los Angeles during the dawn of the HIV/AIDS epidemic.*

Finding fault or blame in other people for things that happen to them is an easy way to feel good about ourselves, and therefore a popular human activity. I was guilty of it myself when I was in my twenties in the early 1980s.

I was a gay man living in West Hollywood, California, and the AIDS crisis was barely on the horizon. I remember hearing about people dying, maybe a friend of a friend, and thinking to myself, "Oh, I think it must be really sleazy people. It's the outlier among us, but not 'us', the good guys." I made the same kind of judgments that would soon be made against my entire gay community. Gay men weren't immune to fear and the self-preservation that comes with it.

But the AIDS epidemic got closer. And closer. The bartender at your favorite club was there on Friday and dead by Monday. The teller at your bank. The guy who lived across the hall.

When the HIV test was approved and released in 1985, it was politically incorrect to take it. There wasn't anything that could come of it that was good. A positive test meant you could be fired, disowned by your family, kicked out of your apartment, and generally treated as a diseased pariah. And there wasn't a single medication to treat it. Why get tested?

Well, because I wanted to know if I should be preparing to die in the next couple of years or sooner. So I took it, and it came back positive.

I lived in a state of mortal fear, every single day, for years. When would I get the spot on my skin, or the cough, or something that would say "The countdown has begun," and I would be dead in a few months? It was hard not to be fatalistic. Why quit smoking? Why plan for retirement?

I had to consider, at the ripe old age of 24, what I wanted my life to mean. I went to work for an AIDS agency that provided emotional support volunteers to people dying of AIDS. It was a sad thing to be doing, but also a very beautiful thing. I had been your basic self-centered, frivolous young man, and I needed to grow up fast.

The fact that I didn't die—and that I managed to survive until effective treatments were discovered more than ten years later—is a complete mystery to me. Life, and HIV, are so random. Many, many people who were inspirational and empowered and had lives of such promise were lost to AIDS anyway. I stopped trying to understand why, and just did my best to live every moment to the fullest and help other people along the way.

Despite everything, I still have joy. I will not allow HIV/AIDS to steal that from me, not anymore. I spend my time telling the story of what happened to us then, because it is a story of resilience in the face of great tragedy, and love and kindness in the face of discrimination and hatred. While people said that AIDS was God's punishment, we were busy caring for one another and starting organizations to feed the sick and provide housing and education and research. In the midst of my community dying, we built and we ministered and we loved. That is a legacy that makes me incredibly proud, and it is a story that must be repeated and remembered.

AIDS has had an enormous influence on the man I have become, but it doesn't define me. If it has taught me anything, it is that we all have our shit. There are people reading this who have been through worse. I am sure of that. But having walked through something this horrific has given me empathy for people unlike myself. I am acutely aware that people struggle, and often in silence.

If I can't take my experience and use it to better understand what you have been through, what the hell was it all for?

COVID Rehab

Alexandra Rendely, MD

Dr Alexandra Rendely is a physical medicine and rehabilitation physician at the University Health Network's Toronto Rehab and a clinician in Quality and Innovation at the University of Toronto. Dr Rendely is a musculoskeletal and sports medicine physiatrist with an inpatient and outpatient practice and a special interest in COVID rehabilitation.

Learning alongside our patients. Learning alongside the world.

COVID rehab was created out of a necessity. The role that rehab plays following an acute COVID-19 infection continues to adapt and shift and has done so since its inception in mid to late 2020.

'Long COVID', 'Long Haulers', 'Post COVID-19 Condition' or 'Post Acute Sequalae of SARS-COV-2' are some of the most common terms used for those experiencing symptoms after the resolution of their acute COVID infection. The terminology, definition and timeline of diagnosis of Post COVID-19 condition depends on who is asked and where the research originated. As we try to hone our understanding of the Post COVID-19 condition, it is most essential that we dispel ourselves of the false notion that we have all the answers. Though we are actively learning and adding to our collective knowledge, there is still so much we do not yet understand. Acknowledging the unknown will prove to be critical as we move forward in navigating this disease.

Is this a post viral reaction? Or is this more on the spectrum of chronic fatigue/myalgic encephalomyelitis? Or is this something else, not yet confirmed by research?

Ongoing research hopes to provide a cohesive definition and timeline to unify those who qualify for this diagnosis and treatment. Currently, the World Health Organization's consensus statement recognizes individuals with probable or confirmed cases that occur three months from the onset of COVID-19 symptoms, who have ongoing symptoms that cannot be explained by an alternative diagnosis.

Physical medicine and rehabilitation physicians have pivoted, along with our allied health colleagues, to become COVID rehab clinicians. While the terms may be new, we have been able to draw on research that has been studied for various other conditions.

With more than 410 million people diagnosed with COVID-19 worldwide in early 2022, the sheer number of individuals who will require rehab following a COVID-19 infection will be astronomic—and continues to skyrocket. Conservative estimates postulate that 10-15% of individuals will have ongoing symptoms three months following infection. That is hundreds of thousands of individuals worldwide who will not be able to return to work, school and hobbies.

Rehab medicine's core values are to help restore function and quality of life. With these principles in mind, we look at every individual, their situation and their goals, and we create a personalized treatment plan to help return them to the activities they enjoy.

Relying on a multidisciplinary team approach, COVID rehab addresses the more than 100 symptoms documented by patients that impact their ability to return to their prior function. Myths that ongoing symptoms only occur from severe infections have been dispelled. Patients with mild, moderate or severe infections are all at risk of Long COVID.

This spans those who required hospitalization and those who did not, those who survived the ICU and those who did not need intubation. Predicting who will have long-term complications and who will not is currently the million-dollar question. Research is continuing to evolve, and finding medical comorbidities, ages or gender-specific identifiers that can stratify patients may lead to earlier treatments and interventions.

For now, COVID rehab must be recognized as an essential part of post COVID recovery. COVID rehab includes those who required an inpatient admission to a rehab ward following hospitalization. These patients tend to present along the lines of post intensive care syndrome (PICS), which makes sense, as there is tremendous overlap. Trying to tease out which parts of a patient's symptoms are from a prolonged ICU admission and which parts come from the lingering effects of post COVID infection can often be a challenge. As the pathophysiology of post COVID is being researched, hopes of more targeted treatments are on the horizon. In the interim, utilizing first principles of rehab medicine has helped this group recover from severe infections and return to walking, eating, talking and breathing independently—with or without required adaptive aids.

At the other end of the spectrum, those who did not require hospitalization and have been classified as having mild COVID are also at risk of ongoing symptoms. These patients have created support groups for one another and coined the term 'long haulers'. With normal blood work and imaging but ongoing symptoms, some feel that their presentation gets dismissed. As a medical community, we must acknowledge that these symptoms are very real to these patients, even though we don't have all the answers. It is okay to say, "I do not know why you are going through this, but let's find strategies to help you cope a little easier." It is imperative that we support those whose symptoms are unrelenting through physical, emotional and psychological treatments.

With compassion, empathy and an open mind, rehab medicine is helping patients recover from long COVID and help return their function and quality of life.

In The End

Psychiatric Illness and Medical Assistance in Dying
Life Extension
Grief
Six Feet Under

Psychiatric Illness and Medical Assistance in Dying

Dr Derryck H Smith

Dr Derryck Smith is a Clinical Emeritus Professor at the University of British Columbia, Department of Psychiatry. He testified in the Carter case and provided expert testimony to the Canadian Parliament on both bills C 14 and C 7.

Over the years, there has been a lot of stigma associated with mental illness—at one time it was even thought to be possession by the devil. In the last several decades, however, psychiatric illness has increasingly been recognized as a medical condition of the human brain. Most doctors do acknowledge the medical nature of psychiatric illness, and this concept seems to have been increasingly adopted by society at large. Nonetheless, when certain topics come up, it becomes clear that despite the seemingly heightened recognition of mental illness as a true medical condition, it is still not viewed in the same light as many other medical conditions. This tension is best illustrated by examining how psychiatric illness is treated when it comes to Medical Assistance in Dying (MAID).

In the Carter v. Canada case, the Supreme Court ruled that under the Canadian Charter of Rights and Freedoms, assisted dying was a 'right provided certain conditions were met'. Before legislation was passed, individual Canadians had to apply to the courts for MAID, an umbrella term that encompasses what has traditionally been known as euthanasia and assisted suicide. We know from rules flowing from the Carter decision that persons with psychiatric illness as their sole diagnosis are eligible for MAID, given the ruling from the Court of Queens Bench in Alberta and the subsequent appeal to the Court of Appeal. The courts granted patient EF the right to MAID on the sole basis of a psychiatric disorder.

Since then, the federal government has been trying to narrow the criteria. In subsequent legislation, Bill C 14, there was no mention of psychiatric illness in regard to MAID. However, a new criterion was introduced: 'natural death has to be reasonably foreseeable'. No doctor fully understood how to interpret this criterion, but it effectively disallowed persons with psychiatric illness from accessing MAID.

More recently, in a Quebec decision the courts found the phrase 'natural death to be reasonably foreseeable' to be unconstitutional and referred that issue back to the government. Subsequently, another piece of legislation, Bill C 7, was passed that now allows two paths to MAID: one where natural death is reasonably foreseeable and one where it is not. A special parliamentary committee is debating how this should apply to psychiatric patients. As of March 2023 MAID will be allowed for psychiatric patients, but the rules are still not in place.

There is divided opinion within the psychiatric community on another issue, and that is whether or not psychiatric illness is ever irremediable. This touches on another criteria in the legislation, which mandates that a condition must be irremediable if MAID is to be an option. Over the course of my practise career, I have certainly seen many patients whose condition failed to improve after many years of treatment. Psychiatrists spend their practise careers trying to prevent suicide, but while some psychiatrists have spoken out in favor of MAID for psychiatric illness, there are other doctors who now think we are promoting suicide. The courts have concluded that psychiatrists can differentiate between suicidal thoughts and a request for MAID.

To me, this is an issue of human rights and the right of individuals to have control over their own life and death. It is likely this issue will again end up back in the courts, and I am confident the judges will continue to recognize the inherent right of a person to decide to end their life, when certain conditions have been met, and be mindful of the need to protect vulnerable populations. There is, however, no evidence that vulnerable populations are at risk of MAID, and in fact it is white, well-educated and financially stable people who appear to primarily access MAID currently.

As legislation becomes more well-defined and other countries around the world continue to expand the parameters of MAID, the inclusion or exclusion of psychiatric illness will be quite telling as to whether society *truly* views mental illness as a medical condition, or whether the medical recognition of psychiatric illness is merely rhetoric.

Life Extension

John K Davis

John K Davis is a professor of philosophy at California State University, Fullerton, and the author of numerous publications on life extension ethics, including New Methuselahs: The Ethics of Life Extension *(MIT Press, 2018).*

Mainstream geroscientists believe it may be possible in the foreseeable future to slow or halt human aging. This is called life extension, and a public conversation about this is well underway in the media and among scientists and ethicists. That conversation is contaminated by some common false preconceptions about life extension.

Life extension doesn't make you immortal

When you get life extension, you live an *extended life*. It's very common, particularly in the media, to characterize extended life as immortality. This is a mistake. An immortal cannot die. Extended life, by contrast, is biologically just like the life we know (aside from aging). Someone living an extended life is just as vulnerable to accident or disease as the average 25-year-old.

Our sense of extended life may be influenced by stories about people who were given immortality by a potion or supernatural intervention, only to find they can't reverse that decision and must live forever, whether they like it or not. (Spoiler alert: they never like it.)

But extended life will not be permanent. For at least the foreseeable future, life extension will require some combination of these: drugs (broadly construed), stem cell therapy and/or genetic engineering. Neither drugs nor stem cell therapy are permanent; you must keep taking drugs and getting your stem cells renewed to maintain their effects. As for genetic engineering, what can be engineered into your DNA can presumably be engineered back out.

Therefore, you can always terminate your life-extending treatments, resume aging, and die if you ever tire of extended life. If you have doubts about extended life, one option is to give it a try and see how it goes.

Assuming you don't check out of extended life and resume aging, how long would you live if you never aged at all after, say, age 25? We can answer this using current actuarial statistics. If we take out all causes of death that are related to aging, leaving only things like accidents, violence and disease, those statistics tell us that the average length of an extended life would be approximately 1,000 years. However, this is only an average. Depending on luck and caution, you might die at 22, or you might live to be 12,022.

If aging is completely halted (and not merely slowed down), extended life will change our relationship with death

First, if aging is completely halted, your odds of death will not be correlated with age. They will be the same at any age. Therefore, you will not be closer to death at age 900 than you were at age 90 or 19. (The 1,000-year life expectancy is, again, merely an average.) At age 900 you have as much time ahead of you as you had at 29.

Second, and for the same reason, when you die you will lose far more time than you do now. For example, instead of losing, say, 10 years when you die at 75, you will lose 1,000 years when you die at 75, 1,000 years when you die at 975, and so on. You will always lose a life expectancy of 1,000 years.

Finally, all this will be elective. You can use life extension or decline to do so; you can stop using it once you start, and after you stop you can start again.

Even if aging and death are beneficial in some ways, that doesn't mean you aren't even better off with extended life

Bioconservatives argue that death is a blessing, and that aging and mortality bring several benefits. By facing death, we develop courage and other virtues, we avoid procrastinating and use our time well, we invest ourselves in the generations that follow us instead of narcissistically focusing on our own survival, and we appreciate the beauty of life because it is so fleeting.

Maybe so. (I have my doubts about some of these arguments, but, for the sake of argument—maybe so.) However, to say there is an upside to mortality is not to say that you are better off without extended life. These arguments leave out half the analysis.

Many of the bioconservative arguments that extended life is a bad life assume that extended life is immortality

Moreover, many of the bioconservative arguments were originally deployed by thinkers in antiquity to show that an *immortal* life is a bad life. According to Lucretius and others, extended life would be boring, lack meaning, lack the virtues that come from facing death, lead to procrastination because we would have all the time in the universe, and so on.

Whether or not these are good reasons to think an immortal afterlife might be bad for us, they are not reasons to think that extended life would be bad for us. In an extended life you can still die at any time, you can stop taking your life extension meds (so to speak) and resume aging, and you will still have plenty of opportunities to develop courage and other virtues by facing up to setbacks and challenges. Extended life is not the immortal existence of a Greek god. It is mortal in every way except the way that involves aging.

If you think you won't want life extension, be patient

Depending on the survey, anywhere from 38.9% to 56% of respondents in the United States and Australia say they would not want life extension if it were available to them. I consider this a false preconception, and believe that, once life extension really is available, we will reconsider. In time, turning down extended life will be as eccentric a choice as giving up sex in favor of lifelong celibacy. Not a choice to criticize, of course—just unusual.

It is easy to declare indifference to death when death is unavoidable. It is quite another to be indifferent when you have a choice. Our acceptance of normal aging may well be an adaptive preference: adapting what we *want* to what we can *get*. When we can get something more, we may prefer something more.

If you're still not convinced, imagine that God appears at the moment of your death and offers you a choice. You can either cease to exist, or you can have an afterlife that is indistinguishable from the life you have now, except that you will be youth-like indefinitely and you can terminate that afterlife whenever you wish. Would you turn God down? If so, would you turn down a more conventional afterlife if he offered one?

You may someday have that choice, and it won't require a god to get it.

Grief

Dr Craig Goldie

Dr Goldie is a Palliative Medicine Specialist practicing in Kingston, Ontario and Assistant Professor/Residency Training Program Director at Queen's University. Research interests include early palliative care, palliative stigma and psychedelics.

One of the hardest aspects to confront when people are facing the end of their life is grief. It takes so many forms and we often do not have the language to recognize it. People who are experiencing grief may be labelled as anxious, or depressed, or angry, or irritable, or defeated. It affects patients, families and other caregivers alike, including those of us who provide health care services to them.

Grief can occur long before someone dies; it starts at diagnosis and morphs through the many changes that occur with a life-threatening illness: the loss of energy and appetite, weakness and muscle loss, changes in family roles, loss of employment, confronting a much shorter life expectancy, the dying process, and bereavement afterwards.

Perhaps a sentiment that has been overly ingrained in society is that grief should look a certain way and last a certain finite amount of time. When we think of grief, we often imagine someone with a somber expression or tears streaming down their face; and when someone *doesn't* fit this mold, others might view it as strange and even suggest that the person isn't grieving *properly*. Others might also feel like grief is lasting *too long* and the grieving person needs to "get on with life" and "move on".

The truth is, grief manifests very differently for different people. It can be aggressive: anger, hypervigilance, unreasonable expectations for healthcare outcomes. It can be passive: avoidance, minimizing of symptoms, unwillingness to discuss prognosis or the future. It can be caring: trying to 'force-feed' a patient with cancer anorexia so they get stronger, or trying to get them walking/socializing when they are profoundly fatigued. All of these are understandable but can be difficult to navigate.

Since grief is hard to recognize and not part of our regular language, it's important to name it, and discuss it. It's really helpful to give patients and families some tools. I recommend two books for patients and their families: *Lap of Honour: a no fear guide to living well with dying* is written by an experienced counsellor and palliative medicine physician from Vancouver and provides some very practical and non-medical points for patients and families. *What Dying People Want: Practical Wisdom for the End of Life* was written by a Canadian family physician after completing his PhD in the area. There are many others, including child-specific resources, at a website run by Canadian Virtual Hospice: KidsGrief.ca.

It's also very important to recognize that helping to identify and support grief is important both within and outside the medical field. Everyone who deals with end-of-life, from physicians, nurses and personal support workers to spiritual care providers and social workers, to environmental and nutrition service workers, all benefit from understanding grief. It is not something to suppress, nor is it something that is consistent. Like many things in life, grief can ebb and flow and come out at very strange times and in strange ways. We owe it to each other to embrace grief as part of love and to make space for it with understanding and care.

Six Feet Under

Emily Bootle

Emily Bootle is a death care advocate and funeral director in Vancouver, BC. She is a partner at KORU Cremation | Burial | Ceremony where she supports her community with their needs following a loss. Emily is passionate about cultivating death literacy and improving sustainability in her industry.

As a funeral director, I deal with death on a daily basis. I speak with grieving families and help them navigate difficult decisions. I review options of burial versus cremation, facilitate funerals, embalm bodies of the deceased and prepare them for viewings.

Many people probably find it strange when they hear what I do for a living. I'm aware that funeral directors are anomalies in our desire to work so closely with the dead. But contrary to what one might think, it is a misconception that the public was always so detached from death as it is today. It is only more recently in our history that we have siloed the care of our dead into a profession.

Death used to happen in the home, much like birth—the two ends of the cycle. As our medical system evolved, death, like birth, slowly moved out of the home and the community and into institutions. Not surprisingly, we became less comfortable with something that's actually a really natural part of life.

Because of the way our culture has evolved, we easily become scared of our loved ones after death. We no longer view them as the same people they were. Even though the body is that of a loved one, we have a tough time seeing them as that same person. They become a dead body, and that can feel scary. But, in reality, they are still there, and they usually still look quite like themselves. The features might relax, and the smells might change, but they are the same person. No matter what has happened to someone before they died, the image of death and the reality of someone's body is akin. It looks like being extraordinarily relaxed. There's no tension. There's no fear. There's nothing that isn't expected once life has ended.

I view it as an incredible privilege to be the last person to be laying eyes on an individual, no matter who they are, whether they are beloved by many or known by few. And I would see it as an enormous honour if I were able to share that privilege with others, if they were open to it. When families do come to me and want to see their person, or they want to be the one that dresses them and takes part in the body's preparation, my arms are wide open. I hand the reins over completely, because in our deep lizard brains, we know exactly what to do when someone dies. The story we've been told that we don't know what to do is just that—a story. When families do spend time with their loved ones, it can be very empowering. It can transform a lot of their grief. It doesn't eliminate it, but it changes their relationship to it.

In addition, visualizing the body can really help confirm for people that the deceased is actually dead. It might sound strange, but when someone dies in our community, they are essentially taken away; we sort of 'disappear' people. In a hospice or retirement home, when someone dies, we sneak them out the back door or out of the basement. Residents go to bed one night and wake up the next morning to an empty room, from which someone has disappeared. But I think, psychologically, our brains evolve a lot differently than our culture does. I think there is something that kind of clicks into place when you see someone's body and are able to truly acknowledge and accept their death.

It is natural that people fear death. But perhaps what is equally natural is our ability to confront death. Comfort with death need not be unique to funeral directors; it can be accessible to everyone, and with greater openness, perhaps our overall relationship to both our own mortality and the mortality of our loved ones can become more meaningful.

Conclusion

Our lives are filled with, and sometimes even predicated on, preconceptions. In many ways, it is no fault of our own; preconceptions are often the innocent by-product of living in a society with established norms and belief systems, many of which are positive. But if there is one thing I have learned from my time working on *Preconceived*, it is that I can at least do a better job of trying to evaluate whether I subscribe to something because it's the preconception, or whether it truly fits with my values and perspectives. Are my choices merely based on following the status quo, or do they reflect my own introspection and authentic exploration of this complicated world?

Shedding our preconceptions is no easy task. It can be exhausting, time-consuming, and, frankly, overwhelming. But maybe the first step is not to shed our preconceptions, but at least to be cognizant that they exist. If we can be aware of the many preconceptions that shape our lives, we might be surprised by our capacity for growth and change, one tiny step at a time.

If you've enjoyed exploring some of the preconceptions highlighted in this book, I encourage you to continue the journey with me as I interview more guests on an array of new topics on my podcast of the same name, *Preconceived*. You can find it on Apple Podcasts, Spotify, or at www.preconceivedpodcast.com.

Donations

The proceeds from this book will be going towards the charitable organization Pencils for Kids (P4K). P4K is a volunteer-run Canadian charity. Since 2005, it has changed the lives of thousands of women and children in Niger, one of the poorest countries in the world, with new schools, kindergartens, teacher training, scholarships for girls, the Cooper Sewing Centre, and an income-generating farming program for women, Farmers of the Future (FOF). It is also opening the first training school for horticultural technicians in the country, called the Dov Centre.

In 2021, 46 children aged 3-5 died when fires destroyed their kindergartens, which were made of straw. As a result, children of this age are no longer allowed to attend any kindergarten in Niger that is made of straw. To address this tragedy and encourage education, P4K has launched Project Kindergarten to rebuild many kindergartens out of cement and give the opportunity to thousands of children to continue with their education. 100% of the profits from this book will go towards Project Kindergarten in its pursuit to rebuild kindergartens.

www.pencilsforkids.com

Acknowledgements

First and foremost, I would like to thank the authors in this book for taking the time and effort to contribute their vignettes. Needless to say, this book would not have been possible without your participation, and I am immensely grateful for your willingness to share your incredible stories and insights.

Thank you to my copy editor, Alison Thompson, AKA The Proof Fairy. You guided me gracefully through the book editing and publishing process and provided valuable insights on how to bring this project to life. You were an absolute joy to work with.

And lastly, thank you to my amazing family and friends, who have supported me on this journey of starting a podcast and publishing a book. You mean everything to me.

Manufactured by Amazon.ca
Acheson, AB